'A brief … and brilliant biography, a masterpiece of compression and telling detail informed by the distilled wisdom of one of our leading historians … He shows how Churchill's romanticism, determination and love for the English language infused both the British nation and much of the rest of the world with his own passionate view of history and what it means to be fully human'

Alan Judd, *Daily Telegraph*

'Among many recent books on Sir Winston Churchill, John Keegan's stands out as a model of concision and insightfulness about an immense historical personality who helped to shape the world we live in'

Economist

'Keegan's admiration for his subject is rooted in Churchill's command of language: the great wartime speeches which rallied the British people in the face of defeat … a fast-moving and perceptive narrative biography'

David Goodall, *The Tablet*

'Unashamedly laudatory, a history of a "magnificent life". But it gives readers … an insight into not only Churchill's greatness but why others saw the greatness in him'

Contemporary Review

'John Keegan's biography is … very good … good on Churchill the man of peace and he writes sensitively of his two driving passions, History and Liberty'

Geoffrey Best, *History Today*

John Keegan was for many years Senior Lecturer in Military History at the Royal Military Academy, Sandhurst. Since 1986 he has been Defence Editor of the *Daily Telegraph*. He is the author of many books, including *The Face of Battle, Six Armies in Normandy, Battle at Sea, The Mask of Command, The Second World War, The First World War* and *A History of Warfare*. He is a Fellow of the Royal Society of Literature. He received an OBE in the Gulf War honours list and was knighted in 2000. He is married and lives in Wiltshire.

CHURCHILL
JOHN KEEGAN

PHOENIX

A PHOENIX PAPERBACK

First published in Great Britain in 2002
by Weidenfeld & Nicolson
This paperback edition published in 2003
by Phoenix,
an imprint of Orion Books Ltd,
Orion House, 5 Upper St Martin's Lane,
London WC2H 9EA

First published in the USA in 2002 by Viking/Penguin

Second impression 2003

A CIP catalogue record for this book
is available from the British Library.

ISBN 1 84212 530 3

Printed and bound in Great Britain by
Clays Ltd, St Ives plc

CONTENTS

CHURCHILL

1 Churchill and History

CHURCHILL, TO THOSE who were young in the wartime years, could seem a figure of exaggerated stature. The young seek heroes, and – to this schoolboy citizen of a Britain besieged – the Prime Minister seemed anything but heroic. Heroes strode the streets in khaki or navy or air force blue, lean, fit, laughing, recently returned from battle or ready to depart. Churchill, in his shapeless siren suit and comic stove-pipe hat, signatory cigar wedged between flabby fingers, looked wholly unsoldierly. The adulation of adults irritated: 'Winston, good old Winston.' A schoolboy in wartime Britain did not want an old Winston but a young Winston, someone as dashing as the pilots who flew from the local airfields, the commandos who sprinted in training down the local lanes, the torpedo-boat captains who sailed from the local ports to do battle in the narrow seas. Portly Winston, with his jowls and grating voice, appeared a poor fellow beside such paragons.

The Winston of the postwar years was worse. There was ungraciousness in his response to the people's will, which turned him out of office in 1945, an aura about him of the bad loser. Whatever their parents' political opinions, whatever their own, the young could not help but be touched by the excitement of the social revolution the winning Labour party promised. Churchill the opposition politician put the worst possible face on the socialism it preached. The young took the offers of socialism at face value. A free health service for all sounded self-evidently a good thing, as did school and university scholarships for the clever and hardworking, irrespective of parental ability to pay; better state pensions for the old and the poor; new housing for slum dwellers; and secure employment for the survivors of the prewar slump. The Labour party said that it stood for a better Britain, and the young believed. Churchill's warning that a socialist Britain would be worse aroused disbelief, at least among the generation of the future.

I was a member of that generation and remained quite immune to the Churchillian legend throughout my school and university years. Churchill was returned to office in 1951 and, despite several setbacks to his health – one almost disabling – remained Prime Minister until 1955. His was an extraordinary display of recovery and resilience. He was succeeded by his political son and heir, Anthony Eden, who brought with him into ministerial appointments many of the younger men who had learned their political trade in junior appointments during Churchill's wartime premiership. Despite that rejuvenation, Eden's continuation of Churchillian postwar government failed to appeal to the new electorate. He and his colleagues seemed to them heavily Conservative in the old-fashioned sense: traditionally imperialist abroad, selfishly capitalist at home. 'Suez,' as the British still call the attempt in 1956 to reimpose semicolonial control over the Suez Canal and the state of Egypt, through which it runs, seemed the touchstone of last-gasp Churchillianism. The Suez crisis divided the country. To the older, the military attack may have seemed a proper reassertion of the imperial power that Britain was entitled to exercise by virtue of its history; to the young, it appeared a crass attempt at exerting an imperial authority that belonged to its historical past. One way or another, the failure at Suez marked the termination of the overseas epic of which Churchill, throughout his long life, had been standard-bearer. Suez spoke *finis* to all for which Churchill had stood.

Such, certainly, was my outlook as I came to the end of my education. Then, in a hot summer in New York City in 1957, a chance episode transformed my appreciation of the states-man under whom I had grown up. I had begun a journey through the United States, funded by a philanthropic American graduate of my Oxford college. I was waiting to join another beneficiary of the traveling scholarship he had established. It was the first time I had been by myself in a foreign country, previous expeditions to France having been spent with schoolmasters or family friends. The apartment I had been lent overlooked Union Square, then the centre of a drab commercial district. The owners were away, and I knew no one in the city. I was, for a few days, at a loose end, lonely, and – in a post-adolescent way – depressed and disoriented. America was unsettling, materially so much smarter and more modern than backward, war-worn Britain; spiritually so much more energetic and self-confident. The Britain I had left a few weeks before was undeniably in decline, the America I had entered so evidently booming, in wealth and in enjoyment of world power. My absent hosts belonged, moreover, to the American elite: the Ivy League, the *Social Register*, the chic world of New York intellectual life. The class of which they were members was about to inherit the earth, while mine, after a century of global dominance, was taking its farewell.

I found, among their stock of long-playing records – another novelty to this British visitor – music to indulge self-induced melancholy, such as Beethoven's *Eroica* and Bruckner's Seventh Symphony. The heavy chords reinforced the lethargy that came with unfamiliar semi-tropical heat. Then I turned up something else: a record called *The War Speeches of Winston Churchill*. What on earth, I asked myself, was anything so un-chic, ponderous, and pompous doing among the possessions of smart New Yorkers? What could the ex-Prime Minister's long, punctuated periods have to say to them? Out of pure curiosity – for I was too young to remember Mr Churchill in 1940 – I put the disc on the turntable and began to listen.

The effect was electrifying. The needle chose the track of Churchill's speech of May 19, 1940, broadcast to the nation by the BBC. The voice was instantly recognizable. The power, the inspiration of his words was not. 'I speak to you for the first time as Prime Minister,' he began. Today I can recite the passage by heart; then it came to me with the same force as it must have done to his anxious listeners in the disastrous days of the Battle of France, when the Third Republic was about to give up the ghost and the British Expeditionary Force (BEF) was already in full retreat to Dunkirk. 'I speak to you for the first time as Prime Minister [pause] at a solemn hour in the life of our country, of our

Empire, of our Allies, and above all of the cause of freedom.'
Three heavy beats – 'country,' 'Empire,' 'Allies' – and the
dramatic rallentando: 'cause of freedom.'

I felt my spine stiffen. Then the voice changed tempo,
from rallentando to recitative:

A tremendous battle is raging in France and Flanders. The
Germans [Churchill had a way of pronouncing the word
German that combined menace with contempt] by a remarkable
combination of air bombing and heavily armoured tanks
['remarkable' was a Churchillian adjective that often conveyed
contempt also – 'a remarkable example of modern art' was his
verdict on the Graham Sutherland portrait of himself presented
by Parliament in 1954] have broken through the French defences
north of the Maginot Line, and strong columns of their
armoured vehicles are ravaging the open country, which for the
first day or two was without defenders. They have penetrated
deeply and spread alarm and confusion in their track.

Behind them there are now appearing infantry in lorries, and
behind them, again, the large masses are moving forward.

Even as the crisis pressed upon Churchill the Prime Minister,
Churchill the soldier could not resist recounting the sweep and
drama of military manoeuvre, with brilliant if chilling effect.

Then the mood changed again, to a call for national unity:
'We have differed and quarrelled in the past; but now one
bond unites us all – to wage war until victory is won, and
never to surrender ourselves to servitude and shame,
whatever the cost and agony may be.' Finally, there was a
promise: 'Conquer we must; conquer we shall.'

The record ran on, as I leaned on the window sill in the

heavy heat of a New York June evening. There followed the speech of June 18, 1940, delivered on the same day that the exiled de Gaulle made an appeal to his own people to fight for a free France and to believe in final victory. Churchill was in bulldog mood:

Hitler [there was a spluttery, glottal pronunciation of that name, which was to become familiar] knows that he will have to break us in this island or lose the war. If we can stand up to him [echoes of *Vitai Lampada*, the Victorian poet Henry John Newbolt's epic of schoolboy sportsmanship, which had inspired more of the British than might care to admit to it] all Europe may be free and the life of the world may move forward into broad, sunlit uplands. But if we fail, then the whole world, including the United States … will sink into the abyss of a new Dark Age… Let us therefore brace ourselves to our duties and so bear ourselves that if the British Empire and its Commonwealth last for a thousand years, men will still say, '*This* was their finest hour.'

I was suffused with an unaccustomed sense of pride in country, and then with pride in common citizenship with a man who, at a time when ordinary mortals might have looked for accommodation with an overpowering enemy, could feel such courage and call for equal courage from those he led. That he represented the spirit of true leadership I thereafter had no doubt. The themes were constant. Those thrown down as a challenge in the darkest days, when Hitler's army loomed across the Channel, were repeated at every stage through the war's five years, recounted in the words the record repeated: *hardship* and *agony*, but also *sunshine* and *hope* and the promise eventually of *conquest* and *victory*. In his first speech as Prime Minister to the House of Commons he had offered only 'blood, toil, tears and sweat,' but he had proclaimed almost in the same breath a policy and an aim of breathtaking scope. 'You ask: What is our policy? I will say: It is to wage war by sea, land and air with all our might... You ask: What is our aim? I can answer in one word: Victory! Victory at all costs, victory in spite of all terror, victory however long and hard the road may be.' That was said on May 13, 1940. On June 4 he made to the Commons the most celebrated speech of his life. The evacuation of the BEF from the beaches of Dunkirk was just reaching its end; its soldiers had recrossed the Channel with little more than their rifles, leaving behind all the heavy equipment – guns, tanks – needed to meet an invasion of Britain by the Wehrmacht. There were no replacements at home, no reserves, no fortifications. A citizen militia, the Home Guard, belatedly called into being, was equipping itself with pitchforks and pikes. Heavy bombing was imminently anticipated, a cross-Channel armada of German landing craft expected at any moment. The island was effectively defenceless. By any objective assessment defeat stared Britain in the face, and all rational judgement was for making peace on any conditions offered. Churchill, however, rejected capitulation in absolute terms.

'We shall not flag or fail,' he insisted. 'We shall go on to the end ... We shall defend our island, whatever the cost may be. We shall fight on the beaches, we shall fight on the landing-grounds, we shall fight in the fields and in the streets, we shall fight in the hills. We shall never surrender.' Those who heard those words, it is said, never forgot anything about them: the rhythm of his sentences, the timbre of his voice, above all the magnificently defiant 'never' of 'We shall never surrender.' They were electrified; and that sensation, transferred by word of mouth from Members of Parliament to common people, began the process that Isaiah Berlin, the Oxford philosopher, was to identify as the imposition of Churchill's 'will and imagination upon his countrymen.' It was transmitted 'with such intensity that in the end they approached his ideals and began to see themselves as he saw them.'

How did he see them? Churchill the aristocrat was also Churchill the populist; in either guise he was always, close beneath the skin, Churchill the romantic. He romanticized the history of his country and, in so doing, easily romanticized its people. Churchill the subaltern, as a young officer of the 4th Hussars, had known Kipling's Tommy Atkins, the long-service private soldier of Empire. Kipling's *Soldiers Three* – Learoyd, Ortheris, Mulvaney (the dour Yorkshireman, the cynical Cockney, the wayward Irishman) – were Churchillian familiars. He must, as Kipling did, have perceived their defects: social surliness, chauvinism, contempt for racial inferiors. He also perceived their virtues: patriotism, loyalty even to resented superiors, courage, and the prevailing value of fair play. His acquaintance with the working-class Tories of the constituencies he had contested in his youth, Oldham, Manchester, Dundee, reinforced his belief in the devotion of the British to the idea of their own United Kingdom. As a soldier he learned of British manliness. As the son, beloved charge, and husband of strong women – Jennie Jerome Churchill, Mrs Elizabeth Everest, Clementine Hozier, the first an American who had made herself British – he had come to understand the deep Britishness of the opposite sex,

Britishness to him standing for courage, tenacity, and an ultimate moral decency.

Hence the recurring themes of his great wartime speeches: the call to sacrifice, the warning of hardships in store – 'the British,' he said in June 1941, 'are the only people who like to be told how bad things are' – and, repeated time after time, even when it defied reality, the promise of victory. On May 13, 1940, three days after the great German offensive in the West had opened with disastrous effect on the Anglo-French armies, he had proclaimed the aim of 'victory at all costs, victory in spite of all terror, victory however long and hard the road may be.' On May 9, 1945, the day five years later when victory was finally proclaimed in Europe, he spoke from a balcony in Whitehall to salute the crowds below: 'God bless you all! This is *your* victory … Everyone, man or woman, has done their best. Neither the long years, nor the dangers, nor the fierce attacks of the enemy, have in any way weakened the independent resolve of the British nation. God bless you all!' The promised victory had been brought home, and he at once gave it as a thanks offering to the people. Yet it was quite as much his as theirs – without his determination, conceived at the conflict's outset and sustained throughout its long and turbulent course, to 'wage war'; without his conviction, during the eighteen months of 'standing alone', that allies would be found to redress the balance of German military power; without his belief that evil would not triumph over good and that his country embodied virtue; without his restless energy and relentless will, the harvest of victory would not have been brought in. 'I was brought up', he told the US Congress in December 1941, 'in my father's house to believe in democracy. "Trust the people," was his message.' On becoming leader of the Conservative party in December 1940, he also said, 'I have always faithfully served two public causes ... the maintenance of the enduring greatness of Britain ... and the historical continuity of our island life.' He had certainly trusted the people and taught them to trust him. On that trust, given and won, the historical continuity of British life had been assured.

The idea of history – as he knew and perceived it – had by 1940 come to suffuse Churchill's being. It now supplies the key to any understanding of his behaviour, mature character, and even personality. Certainly little else suffices; Churchill's inner life would otherwise remain a mystery. He was not religious. 'King and country,' his doctor, Lord Moran, recorded, 'was about all the religion Winston had.' That did not mean that he was unmoved by either the moral or the spiritual. On the contrary, he had a profound moral sense and deep spiritual feelings. Neither, however, had a metaphysical basis. He altogether lacked an interest in abstractions, philosophical as well as political, and was not introspective. His beliefs were therefore instinctive rather than the product of private reflection, conventional and inherited rather than derived from debate over first principles, as they might have been had he had a university education.

Churchill had had, partly through his own fault, very little education at all. His beliefs had simple origins, in the piety and goodness of his beloved nanny, Mrs Everest; in the code of schoolboy fair play; in the ethic of manliness learned at the Royal Military College (RMC) at Sandhurst and in his regiment; in the strictures of the Commandments, preached in the Old Testament language that was to be one of the strongest of influences on his own, in Harrow School chapel. From all those sources Churchill derived an undoubted sense of sin; his horror of wrongdoing was to inform his political life, particularly as it brought him eventually to confront the crimes of the dictators. He appears, however, to have carried no burden of personal sinfulness, that besetting affliction of thinking Victorians, perhaps because his physical nature exempted him from sexual temptation, the cause of much Victorian neurosis. Churchill, as he himself recognized with uncharacteristic insight, had a weak sexual drive. He was innocent in his judgment of others' sexuality and apparently personally innocent of sexual experience until his marriage, at the age of thirty-four, to Clementine Hozier, herself serenely pure-minded. Churchill was a moral oddity: a man who was worldly-wise without being a man of the world. It may have been his indifference to the lures of the flesh that heightened his susceptibility to the seduction of words and to the spell of history conceived as romance.

If challenged, Churchill might have said that his morality derived from historical universals and his spirituality from humanist tradition. The mature Churchill, however, was not challenged. Deliberately or not, as the years went on, he avoided intimacy, outside his intense but essentially secret relationship with Clemmie, as much imperious mistress as cherished wife. He did not confide, he did not confess – except to the emotion of public setback, which he could discuss with comrades in political life. Comrades, moreover, were not friends. Indeed, Churchill's life is remarkable for its paucity of friendships: few in youth, eventually none at all. Of friendship he often spoke, but those supposed to be friends – particularly the 'three Bs', lawyer and politician Lord Birkenhead (F. E. Smith), newspaper magnate Lord Beaverbrook (Max Aitken), and his parliamentary private secretary Brendan Bracken – Clemmie rightly identified as at best collaborators, at worst cronies. She disapproved strongly of their influence on him, which she correctly recognized as encouraging his regrettable tendency to boastfulness and rash judgment.

Real friends might have tempered those faults in reasoned conversation. Churchill did not allow it. He loved company, but he talked to command attention and to win. As his life drew out, moreover, and increasingly during the lonely years before his sudden elevation to the premiership ensured the attention of every ear, conversation increasingly became monologue, to listeners chosen because of their ability to keep silent or express agreement with his views. Theirs was not an ordeal. Churchill's exposition of his views was eloquent, arresting, allusive, often very funny. It was his own views in which he was interested, however, not the responses of others.

Those views were drawn above all from his lifelong reading of British history and his own writing of it in later life, particularly *The World Crisis* and his four-volume biography of his great ancestor, Marlborough. Completed before his accession to office as prime minister in 1940, each concerned Britain's struggle to achieve or sustain its status as a great power during a major conflict, the War of the Spanish Succession, 1701–14, and the First World War, respectively. He had, however, already during the 1930s embarked on a much larger undertaking, *A History of the English-Speaking Peoples*, which – though it was not to be completed for twenty years

– had allowed him to begin thinking of the historical processes that had formed not only his own country, but also his mother's American homeland, in the widest terms. He saw them, justifiably, as intimately intertwined. Perception of that relationship, sometimes hostile, sometimes merely aloof, but always and of its nature indissoluble, was to determine the direction of his career as politician and statesman in the last and most important phase of his public life.

Famously, Charles de Gaulle begins his memoirs with the declaration: 'I have always had a particular idea of France.' Churchill, similarly, had a particular view of Britain, and his ultimate indulgence of the pretensions of the leader of Free France may have been founded on a recognition that they had a common historical outlook: a devotion to the idea of national identity as an absolute value. Churchill loved France and admired its great men, particularly Georges Clemenceau and Joseph Foch, with whom he had waged the First World War; but he loved France as a place of wartime adventure and of subsequent distraction and pleasures, above all painting. His feelings for his own country were different altogether: fierce, protective, dutiful, proud. De Gaulle's were no doubt closely similar. While his war memoirs, however, when they eventually appeared, were essentially an explanation of how a great nation had preserved its spirit despite defeat, Churchill had another story to tell when he came to write *The Second World War*: how a great nation, often threatened by tyrants, had in the severest of its ordeals staved off defeat and emerged once again victorious. De Gaulle's war memoirs are a magnificent apology, Churchill's a paean of triumph.

Yet he indulges in no self-aggrandizing. Hold great office though he did, it was the greatness of others that he sought to proclaim, the greatness above all of the British people, stalwart and uncomplaining, and of the country to which they belonged. Churchill saw Britain as the incarnation of its own history, told in terms of its institutions, laws, and achievements. Its institutions he venerated, Parliament above all. Its laws he saw as the means by which Parliament, and therefore the people, gave force to the fundamental principles on which their society was founded: the freedom of the individual, the sanctity of justice, the limitation of the power of the state. Britain's achievements – the defeat of Continental imperialists, the foundation of its own Empire, victory over European warlords and dictators – he viewed as the process by which its constitutional values were enforced in the international arena and transmitted to the wider world.

Churchill's historical vision was simple and direct – too simple to be taken seriously by professionals. Professional historians see complexities and ambiguities; Churchill saw certainties. Those certainties derived directly from the sources he used to teach himself the island's story, historians Henry Hallam, W. E. H. Lecky, Thomas Babington Macaulay, champions all of the Whig view that British life broadened down from precedent to precedent, each precedent an advance toward the desired ends of life, liberty, and the pursuit of happiness, on which the Whig fathers of his mother's country had founded their commonwealth. They derived also from the mighty rhythms of the prose in which he learned the history he loved, made it his own, and transmitted it to his people in literature and rhetoric. No influence was more pervasive than the prose of Edward

Gibbon, whose opening epitome of the Antonine age furnished him with his vision of how enlightened empire might transform the future of mankind. No influence was stronger on his mode of thought than the prose of the Old Testament, through which the epic of a warrior people covenanted with God had been given to the world. In the end the personality of Churchill and the prose that inspired his being so interpenetrated each other as to be indistinguishable and mutually inextricable. The inner voice of words shaped his thought and determined his choices. Prose was deed, prose was outcome. Churchill the war leader was literature in action and written history in realization. When the terrible ordeal of conflict was over, the magnificent language of Exodus and *The Decline and Fall of the Roman Empire* welled up into an epitome of his own and his nation's life, in his speech to the Commons at the moment of victory:

Once again the British Commonwealth and Empire emerges safe, undiminished and united from a mortal struggle. Monstrous tyrannies which menaced our life have been beaten to the ground in ruin, and a brighter radiance illumines the Imperial Crown than any which our annals record. The light is brighter because it comes not only from the fierce but fading glow of military achievements but because there mingle with it in mellow splendour the hope, joys and blessings of mankind. This is the true glory, and long will it gleam upon our forward path.

The glow of military achievement and the splendour of empire have almost faded away, but a true glory continues to gleam over Churchill's life, works, and words.

2 Family and Youth

CHURCHILL WAS BORN, on November 30, 1874, into the inner circle of Victorian society and yet began life as an outsider, as he was to remain for much of his career. His family, of which the seventh duke of Marlborough was then head, was one of the greatest in England. The first duke, John Churchill, had been deluged with wealth and honours for his command of the British armies against France in the War of the Spanish Succession. Parliament had voted the money to build him the family seat, Blenheim Palace, named after his greatest victory, and it was almost unequalled for size and the splendour of its contents even in a Victorian Britain filled with the mansions of rich and ancient families. Neither Wellington nor Nelson – though their victories at Waterloo and Trafalgar over Napoleon greatly exceeded those of Marlborough in strategic importance – was so sumptuously rewarded. Neither Wellington's nor Nelson's descendants came to occupy a place in British society equivalent to that held by his. The Marlboroughs became grandees from the grant of the original ducal title and remained so despite every vicissitude that afflicted their line.

The vicissitudes were many and successive. Other English

families raised to great place, the Cecils being the prominent example, bred true to the achievements of the founder. The Churchills, however, seemed to transmit bad blood. It may have come from the first duke himself, whom David Cannadine, the premier historian of the British aristocracy, has described as 'a man of dubious political and personal morality' who had 'betrayed James II, conspired against William III and pursued power and wealth with unscrupulous and single-minded ardour.' He was, nevertheless, formidable; the inheritors of the title were not. 'The third, fourth and fifth dukes,' Cannadine writes, 'were profligate even by the standards of the late eighteenth and early nineteenth centuries,' and 'unstable, depressive and bad-tempered' to boot. Winston's grandfather, the seventh duke, broke the pattern. Like many other noblemen of the High Victorian age, he conformed to the religious piety of the era and to the ethic of aristocratic responsibility, values reinforced by his marriage to a strong-willed daughter of Lord Londonderry. The extravagance of his ancestors, however, nullified his efforts to restore the Marlborough fortunes. Though he managed to retain Blenheim – still in Marlborough hands today, its beauties protected by its recognition as a World Heritage Site – he was forced to sell outlying estates to settle inherited debts, together with the Marlborough jewels and the Blenheim library. His son, the eighth duke, Winston's uncle, reverted to disreputable type. He sold the Blenheim collection of old masters for the then extraordinary sum of £350,000 (perhaps fifty million dollars today), but even that refreshment of family funds did not stem the outflow. Nor did his second marriage, after a scandalous divorce, to an American heiress. His successor, Sunny, who became the ninth duke in 1892, also married an American heiress, a Vanderbilt no less, but neither the marriage nor her infusion of wealth brought him luck. Twice divorced, Sunny died, almost insolvent, at the end of a life in which he had been refused reception at court by both Edward VII and his son George V.

Sunny was Winston's cousin. Winston's father, Lord Randolph Churchill, also married an American heiress, Jennie Jerome, whose father was a stockbroker and part-owner of the *New York Times*. It was an era of alliances between rich American beauties and titled British gentlemen. American money was desired, quite cynically in Sunny's case, to rescue once great families from the consequences of extravagance. British titles were sought as ornaments to vulgar fortune. In some cases the exchange worked. Mary Leiter, of Chicago, became Lady Curzon, beloved and loving wife of a future viceroy of India. In Lord Randolph's case it did not. Jennie, a sensational beauty, soon found other men more attractive than her husband, who in any case had been syphilitic since youth and was to die of the tertiary symptoms. Randolph, compulsively extravagant (horses, cards, but above all the expensive game of politics), did not acquire enough money by the marriage to fund his way of life. Theirs may nevertheless have been a love match: Jennie remained powerfully attractive to the opposite sex all her life; Randolph was dynamically masculine. Their relationship was, however, fraught from the start with tension, and they spent much time apart even during Winston's infancy. By the time he began to grow up there were three separate influences on his life: his adored mother, the 'Morning Star'; Mrs Everest, who fulfilled a maternal role the often absent Jennie could not; and his aloof but deeply admired father.

* * *

Randolph Churchill might have been a great Victorian politician. His son, who wrote his biography, thought so, and many others, within and without the Conservative party, did as well. He was an arresting public speaker, and he had ideas – above all the idea that his party, traditionally that of the propertied classes, might become the vehicle of 'Tory democracy'. Had he taken the time, Randolph might have learned the means to revive Disraeli's appeal to the working classes and so to stem the apparently irresistible rise of Gladstonian Liberalism. Randolph, however, had no patience. He was as extravagant in his emotions as his Marlborough ancestors had been with their money. His parliamentary and rhetorical talents quickly won him high office, as Secretary of State for India, then Chancellor of the Exchequer. The second highest position in government did not satisfy him. He wanted to be First Lord of the Treasury, Prime Minister. His superior in the Conservative party, the marquess of Salisbury, head of the Cecil family, which had served the state since the reign of Queen Elizabeth I, was disinclined to cede, even to a colleague whose brilliance as a campaigner could overturn Gladstone's majority in the House of Commons, as Lord Randolph did in the general election of 1886. Lord Randolph thought the triumph entitled him to the Conservative leadership. Salisbury, to whose family attached none of the scandal that adhered to the Churchills, did not. Pious, upright, intellectual, he was supremely assured of his position both in society and politics. He simply ignored Lord Randolph's attempts to unseat him in the months that followed the 1886 election, leaving his antagonist to make his own mistakes. Toward the end of the year Lord

Randolph made the irretrievable mistake of offering his resignation as Chancellor, believing that the challenge would bring Salisbury's downfall. It did not. Lord Randolph's parliamentary colleagues, who supported him so vociferously in the House, declined to stage a parliamentary revolution. In September 1886, at the age of thirty-seven, he found himself without office and thereafter increasingly without influence in the world of politics.

He spent the last six years of his life 'dying by inches in public', in the words of Lord Rosebery, a future Conservative Prime Minister. His interventions in Parliament became an increasing embarrassment as the tertiary symptoms of syphilis took hold, his stutterings and non sequiturs causing his old friends to leave the chamber rather than witness the spectacle of his degradation. His behaviour in private life was equally embarrassing, and his appearance also. His features disintegrated; he wept, slobbered, became incoherent in speech. In his last months Jennie, emotionally faithful to him as she had not been physically since the early years of their marriage, took him on a long sea voyage in the hope of restoring his health. It did no good. Soon after his return he died in London, on January 24, 1895. He was buried in the churchyard of Bladon, a village near Blenheim, where Winston's own grave was to be dug exactly seventy years later.

In the final months of his idolized father's life, Winston, then a cadet at the Royal Military College, Sandhurst, insisted on learning the true nature of the fatal illness, which had thus far been kept from him. The facts were never to alter his feelings for Randolph. At the Bladon funeral he conceived his future task to be 'to lift again the flag I found lying on a stricken field.' Soon he conceived the idea of himself entering

Parliament, 'to pursue his aims and vindicate his memory', as he would later write. The realization of that ambition lay far in the future, though in 1906 he succeeded in having his biography of his father published. In the meantime he was still a 'gentleman cadet', not yet launched on his military career and quite without the funds necessary to transfer to politics. His father's estate, of £76,000, was almost completely consumed by debt, his mother's Jerome income was insufficient to cover her extravagances, and his own starting salary as a second lieutenant was to be only £120 a year. Dreams required substance to realize. In 1895 Winston's future had no material foundation, and he was almost without social or family support.

In April, four months after his father's death, Mrs Everest, his beloved 'Woom', who had cosseted him through childhood and youth, was stricken with peritonitis. The family had cast her off almost without a pension after nineteen years of service. Winston had supported her with small sums. On hearing the news of her last illness, he abandoned his military duties to fetch a doctor, engage a private nurse, and hold her hand in her last hours. He also arranged her funeral, raised a headstone on her grave, and paid a local florist for its upkeep. 'I feel very low,' he wrote to his mother, 'and find I never realised how much old Woom meant to me.'

That was untrue. Churchill venerated Woom's memory all his life. Her picture hung in his bedroom until he died. Like so many nannies to the Victorian aristocracy's children, she had been his real mother, and no one could thereafter fill her place. Jennie, despite her dazzling performance on the stage of family and social life, certainly could not. She may have seemed to her son 'a fairy princess: a radiant being possessed of limitless power and riches,' she may have taken pride in his early successes, filled his request for books during his early military exile in India, and made him political introductions on his return. Her conduct nevertheless made it clear that her real interest was not in her sons (Winston's brother, John Spencer Churchill, had been born in 1880) but in other men. Her affairs became more flagrant after Lord Randolph's death and culminated in her making two unsuitable marriages. In 1899, at the age of forty-five, still a raving beauty, she married a man twenty years her junior. In 1917, when she was sixty-four and a divorcee, she married for the third time, again to a man twenty years younger than herself. When death at last overtook her, in 1922, she was still 'very beautiful and splendid', in Winston's description of her lying at rest: 'All the sunshine and storm of life was over.' She had brought him more storm than sunshine. A boy born into the sort of family that normally supplied the imperial service class, in which he was to make his career, should have been able to count on the support of high-minded, principled parents, wedded to the ideals of duty, honour, country. Instead his family inheritance was of ruthless political ambition on his father's side and frivolous social and sexual self-indulgence on his mother's. Churchill should have gone to the bad. The wonder is that he did not.

What perhaps saved him was the military ethic, which was to guide his path in the aftermath of his father's death. Winston had not been a successful schoolboy. Though he was of lively intelligence, it was not of the exam-passing sort. A Churchill would normally have proceeded to Eton, where the sons of the family had been schooled for six generations. Instead his parents thought at first of the far more academic Winchester. At a late stage they decided instead upon Harrow, apparently for its high and healthy location. The child Winston had been sickly. He had, unfortunately, also failed to acquire a competence in the subjects usually necessary for transition from junior to senior school at the age of thirteen – notably Latin and Greek. In a much-quoted passage from *My Early Life*, he describes his performance on the Harrow Latin entrance exam:

> I wrote my name at the top of the page. I wrote down the number of the question, '1'. After much reflection I put a bracket around it, thus, '(1)'. But thereafter I could not think of anything connected with it that was either relevant or true. Incidentally there arrived from nowhere in particular a blot and several smudges. I gazed for two whole hours at this sad spectacle; and then merciful ushers collected up my piece of foolscap and carried it up to the Headmaster's table.

It had probably already been ordained at Harrow that a son of Lord Randolph Churchill would be admitted whatever his exam results. Despite the blots and smudges on his otherwise blank examination sheet, he was. It was not a promising beginning, and Churchill the Harrovian did little to improve on it. Still, he was not a complete failure at the school. He won a prize for fencing in the English public schools' championship and another at Harrow for reciting many hundred lines of Macaulay's *Lays of Ancient Rome*, the sort of stirring verse that appealed to his romantic temperament. At ordinary and essential subjects – the classical languages,

French, mathematics – he was, however, consistently incompetent, because he patently did not try. He liked history, not then a major examination subject, and he was good at English composition, but his enthusiasm for neither could carry him upward. He was consigned to a sort of remedial class for dullards, in which he remained for three successive sessions. Fortuitously, the master in charge, Robert Somervell, concentrated on the teaching of English language and had a sort of genius in compositional technique. 'Thus,' Winston later wrote, 'I got into my bones the essential structure of the ordinary British sentence – which is a noble thing. And when in after years my schoolfellows who had won prizes and distinctions for writing such beautiful Latin poetry had come down to common English, to earn their living or make their way, I did not feel myself at any disadvantage.'

Disadvantage he was under nonetheless. Official England, in the later Victorian years, demanded success in the conventional subjects, those the founders of the career-on-merit system, Stafford Northcote and Charles Trevelyan, had established as the entry requirement for the foreign, civil, and military services. The Northcote–Trevelyan reforms, inspired by the academic impartiality through which the Chinese emperors had recruited the mandarins, had killed patronage, a system that would in earlier times have ensured Winston's admission to privileged position. By Northcote–Trevelyan standards Winston was doomed to failure. He was bored by the classics, could scarcely calculate, and hated foreign languages. Jennie's insistence that he go to a household in France to learn French – 'No family! No family! Ugh!!' was Winston's response to the order – left him still almost a monoglot. By the age of seventeen he was barely educated.

He had, nevertheless, fixed on a career that required examination results. It was the army. Winston had, since childhood, been fascinated by soldiers and the military life. The army's entrance requirements were lower than those for the Diplomatic, Home, or Indian Civil services. Passing marks were, nevertheless, a necessity for a would-be officer. Winston had, in his last Harrow years, been a member of the school's Army Class, which coached pupils – the duller pupils – in the necessary subjects. Toward the end of his time he had persuaded himself that it had equipped him to pass the competitive exam for which he had been prepared. The persuasion was false. At his first attempt he failed to achieve the marks necessary even for admission to the cavalry, which set the lowest standard. Lord Randolph, who disapproved of the cavalry's reputation for military as well as social frivolity, had hoped for the infantry, leading to a posting in one of the great Mediterranean fortresses – Malta or Gibraltar – where his son would be thoroughly grounded in his profession. At the second attempt Winston did worse, still failing to pass for the cavalry and achieving barely half marks in English composition, the skill on which he prided himself. At the age of seventeen he left Harrow unqualified for any calling and ashamed even to take leave of his schoolfellows.

There was, however, to be a third chance. The dying Lord Randolph agreed that Winston should be sent to a specialist military tutor, Captain Walter James, who ran a cramming establishment in Lexham Gardens in London. James had perfected a technique of anticipating the questions set by the examiners and drilling pupils in the answers. He provided not an education but rote learning. Young Winston's resistance to his methods tested Captain James's patience to the limits; he complained that his pupil tried 'to teach his instructors instead of learning from them'. In the end, however, either his will proved stronger than Winston's or else sense broke in. Winston badly wanted to go to Sandhurst, and in June 1893 he scraped through the entrance exam. His results qualified him only for the cavalry, to his father's disgust, but at least assured him a future.

It was overlooked that his marks in English history vastly exceeded those of any other candidate. Lord Randolph noted only that his son passed in 95th out of 104 new cadets, and was not mollified by the offer of an infantry place when several higher in the list failed to take up theirs. His letters to Winston over the Sandhurst exam were among the most wounding of many reproofs he had written during the boy's adolescence. Winston was cut to the quick. He was further hurt by his father's refusal to make him an adequate allowance; to finance his ownership of a horse, then almost a necessity for an aspiring officer; or to agree that he should have leave to go to London. Winston entered Sandhurst, as he had left Harrow, under the shadow of parental disapproval made clear to his mentors.

To add to his troubles, he was not physically robust. He was only a little over five feet six inches tall and lacked the chest expansion necessary to qualify for graduation. Though he was strikingly redheaded, his pale body was almost hairless, his appearance epicene. He had had a succession of childhood illnesses, including nearly fatal pneumonia, and had an incipient hernia. Moreover, he was accident-prone, as he was to remain for much of his adult life. While preparing for Sandhurst he had, during a boyish game, thrown himself from a bridge, suffering concussion and a ruptured kidney; and later, while holidaying in Switzerland, he had almost drowned when the boat from which he had dived into Lake Geneva was carried off by the breeze. In *My Early Life* he recognized that he had then seen death 'as near as I believe I have ever seen him. He was swimming in the water, whispering from time to time in the rising wind.' As a young officer he would dislocate his right shoulder transferring from ship to shore at Bombay (an injury that remained with him for the rest of his life), dislocate it again playing polo, take a heavy tumble steeplechasing, suffer an indirect gunshot wound while supervising rifle practice, crash while learning to fly, and, in 1931, nearly die when run down by a car in New York City. The jump from the bridge and the swim in Lake Geneva were foolhardy. The circumstances of his other injuries were not. The physical effects, particularly from those suffered at Bombay and on the polo field, suggest inherited lack of strength. Lord Randolph was a puny figure, though of strong will. His son's will was to prove indomitable, but he had little reason to thank his father for the physique he was bequeathed.

The Sandhurst regime of drill, physical training, and equitation eventually helped Winston to overcome his infirmities. He was never to be robust; during the Second World War he succumbed to illnesses that threatened the sure direction of Allied strategy. By the time he passed out of the RMC in December 1894, however, he was a fit young man with, moreover, an excellent cadet record. His place in the order of merit was 20th out of 130, and he had done particularly well in the final exams for tactics, drill, gymnastics, and riding. He had also secured a place in a fashionable cavalry regiment. He had evaded his father's efforts to put him into the 60th Rifles. By his own insistence, and with the help of his mother, who played upon her social connections to achieve that outcome, he had been accepted into the 4th Hussars.

The 4th Hussars were not only smart. Their commanding officer, Colonel John Brabazon, was one of the army's foremost officers, admired by his contemporaries and on personal terms with the royal family. Regimental costs were high. An officer's pay nowhere near met the price of his uniform, horses, mess subscriptions, or necessary social display; but with help from the Blenheim family resources, Winston was quickly launched. By February 1895 he had settled into the regimental routine of stables, riding school, and squadron administration; taken up polo; and begun steeplechasing in his own racing colours.

The regiment was shortly to leave for India, to join the British garrison, a regular episode in the life of every unit of the army, except the Household troops. It would be absent for nine years. While preparing to go, officers were free to take their generous allotment of annual leave, including an uninterrupted spell of ten weeks. Winston may already have become bored with routine; he decided to get out of England and find adventure. There was a real war raging in the Caribbean, where Spain was trying to suppress a deep-rooted insurgency in Cuba. He scented the chance to smell powder. He also detected the possibility of earning money and reputation by writing the war up for a British newspaper. Though both were dubious ambitions for a subaltern with his way to make, such considerations deterred Winston not at all. Working on what would become a lifelong principle of dealing only with those at the top, he secured introductions in Cuba from the British ambassador to Spain, permission to join the war from the British commander in chief, and a brief to secure information from the director of intelligence.

Thus covered in all directions, Winston and a fellow subaltern debarked in Cuba, after a visit to the Jerome family and friends in New York, on November 2, 1895. Before the month was out, he and Lieutenant Reginald Barnes had joined one of Marshal Arsenio Martinez de Campos's punitive columns, marching into the interior to meet and defeat the rebels. The pattern of the war in Cuba, already fixed, was to be tragically repeated throughout Europe's colonial possessions for the next hundred years. The Cuban rebels, inspired by the idea of national liberation, were poorly armed and trained but vastly superior to the Spanish forces in knowledge of the terrain. Their tactics were those of skirmish and ambush, and they had no shame about running away if an engagement went against them. They accepted casualties; welcomed enemy atrocities, which drew the population to their side; had no fixed timetable for victory; and used mountain and forest as refuges into which to melt away when confronted or apparently cornered. Mao Zedong would weave such tactics into a philosophy of 'people's war' fifty years later. The Boers would anticipate Mao's methods in South Africa, in a war in which Winston would also participate in 1900. However, in 1895 he encountered the tactics of evasion and delay for the first time at first hand. The encounter was to mark his attitude to military effort for the whole of his life.

The column, commanded by General Juarez Valdez, left a fortified village and quickly made contact with the enemy.

After following up, the two battalions encamped for the night in dense forest, setting out early next morning. They forded a river, in which Churchill took a swim; he was fired on while dressing, his first experience of danger, which he found exhilarating. The column encamped again and was fired upon while asleep. Marching off, it met the rebels occupying an entrenched position on a ridge in open country. It deployed, in orthodox fashion, into open order, achieved supremacy in the exchange of fire, was then frustrated when the rebels retired, into 'impenetrable woods', and retraced its steps to its fortified starting point. Churchill then made his farewells.

His baptism of fire was an experience to be undergone many times in the future by young French officers in Indo-China and Algeria, Americans in Vietnam, his own countrymen in south-east Asia and Africa. On his return to New York, Churchill described the Cubans as 'not good soldiers, but as runners would be hard to beat.' It was the verdict of any regular officer confronted by freedom fighters for a century to come. Freedom fighters, on their home ground in difficult terrain, would drive conventional European armies to distraction. Even when the imperial forces did not resort to terrorist methods of their own, as they so often did, they sought a solution to insurrection in direct action against the populations in which the freedom fighters worked. The recruitment of local militias was one favored riposte; the 'concentration' of rural populations into settlements controlled by the army was another. 'Concentration camps' were a Spanish invention of the Cuban war; the invention was to be repeated in South Africa during the Boer War. Both were ineffective as measures of control.

Churchill indirectly conceded that in his depreciation of the Cuban rebels he had underestimated their strength. 'The nature of the country is against [the Spaniards],' he said, 'and, furthermore, there is too little combination in the movement of their columns … If the insurgents hold out until the spring rains set in, they may yet win.'

The Cubans, with American help against the Spanish empire, both in the Caribbean and the Philippines, did win in the end. Cuba became an independent state. Churchill, who wanted as an alternative to continued Spanish rule an American protectorate over the island, wrote that 'a Cuban government would be equally corrupt, more capricious and far less stable. Under such a government revolutions would be periodic, property insecure, equity unknown.' He was right. Cuba did briefly become an effective American protectorate. In the aftermath its awful politics fulfilled every one of Churchill's predictions. By then, however, his attentions had shifted elsewhere, to India, to the Muslim lands, to South Africa, and to his own country. They were to be enduring preoccupations. Cuba, nevertheless, had introduced Churchill to war. His understanding of its nature was to ramify throughout the rest of his life.

3 The Army, 1894–1900

WINSTON'S MILITARY APPRENTICESHIP, formal at Sandhurst, informal in Cuba, was now over. On entrance to the fellowship of the 4th Hussars, he became a fully-fledged soldier, bound not only to the profession of arms but to a particular military society. The British regiments founded in the Victorian age were an almost unique form of military organization, not only self-selecting and self-governing but also self-perpetuating. They had been modelled, during the military reforms of 1870–80, on the regiments of the German army, then the most successful in the world. They copied the German system of drawing their recruits from a specified geographical area, and in choosing, by regimental scrutiny, their own officers, who thereafter became exclusively their own. British regiments differed in this way: German soldiers were conscripts, returning to civilian life after two years; British soldiers enlisted for seven years and often re-engaged, so that both they and their officers made long-service careers together. A subaltern, such as Winston Churchill, might join with a private who, twenty years later, would be a sergeant when he had become a major. As a result, regiments like the

4th Hussars were not only military units but social families, whose members knew each other on intimate terms and had no other life beyond the bonds of regimental life.

Winston, given a different character, might have settled easily into a cosy hussar regime. Many of his contemporaries did so, making meritorious careers and retiring as respected veterans, honoured in regimental circles and in wider British society. Theirs was a small world, a conventional one, but known and understood. The clergy of the Church of England pursued similar paths through life, as did Oxford and Cambridge dons and masters at the great public schools. They enjoyed the satisfaction of an insider's life, financially ill rewarded but locally esteemed and emotionally secure.

To the pursuit of local esteem and emotional security Winston was temperamentally ill suited. The temptations of insiderism touched him not at all. Even as a newly commissioned subaltern he was seeking a wider stage, a national name, political importance. Promotion from subaltern to captain, captain to major, the eventual pinnacle of regimental command, were to him targets too distant, and too small, to demand his dedication. He had already identified the means to short-circuit the conventional career: journalism and politics. He already knew he could write, in a direct and arresting fashion. His relationship with his father, troubled as it had been, taught him that he had access to a wide circle of potential political supporters. He already sensed that his hussar career was likely to be short-lived. Even as he arrived in India in 1897, bound for the down-country station of Bangalore, he was planning his escape. On November 18, 1896, he wrote to Lady Randolph that 'as a soldier, my intelligent interests are supposed to stop short at Polo, racing and Orderly Officer.' While in India he would play polo with gusto, as he would elsewhere until the age of fifty-two, but he wanted to use his time there at least to acquire 'Indian information and knowledge', to fit him for a future political career; if the chance came to take part in one of British India's frequent frontier wars, where medals and fame could be won, better still. Beyond India beckoned the opportunity of detachment to the Anglo-Egyptian army, poised to recapture the Sudan. Even further distant was England itself, where any successful young soldier stood the chance of picking up a parliamentary seat at a by-election. There were small wars in Africa where a subaltern might win sudden promotion; in 1897 there was to be a Greco-Turkish war in Crete, in which Britain intervened. The North-West Frontier, Egypt, Crete – in steamy, sleepy Bangalore, during 1896–97, Winston fretted to find his way to any of those scenes of strife. Unlike another genius, the young Kipling, who a decade earlier had used Indian exile to feed his imagination and establish his literary reputation, Winston had not the patience to wait. He wanted fulfillment at once, through violent action, not the delayed satisfaction that comes from artistic creation.

Yet Winston did possess a sort of patience, which would bear fruit in later years. In the hot afternoons of the Bangalore cantonment, he set himself to store his mind through a regimen of concentrated reading. Kipling had arrived in India with his reading already done. A boy of extraordinary intellectual maturity, he had already subsumed into his consciousness not only the English classics, including Hakluyt as well as Shakespeare and Milton, but huge tracts of European and American literature, Pushkin and Lermontov but also Whitman and Twain; the French symbolists and decadents were soon to follow. Little of that was to the young Winston's taste. He wanted facts, order, reason. His demands were met by his mother, who sent him expensive books by the crate during his Indian years. The diet was, in its way, as impressive as Kipling's. The mainstay was Gibbon, the greatest of English historians, whom 'through the glistening hours of the Indian day, from … stables till the evening shadows proclaimed the hour of Polo, I devoured.' Even before finishing all eight volumes of Gibbon, however, he had embarked on Plato's *Republic* and then the twelve volumes of Macaulay's *History of England*, 'fifty pages of Macaulay and twenty-five of Gibbon every day.' Shortly afterward he launched into Schopenhauer, Malthus, Darwin, Aristotle's *Politics*, Pascal, Saint-Simon, and Adam Smith. He also asked his mother for the hundred volumes of the *Annual Register*, the record of British public life since the publication had been founded by Edmund Burke. He received only twenty-seven, even the spendthrift Jennie shrinking from the expense, but he appears to have consumed the lot, with the object of building up 'a scaffolding of logical and consistent views which will perhaps tend to the creation of a logical and consistent mind.' The suspicion that his requests were Winstonian showing off is negated by the obvious effect of his reading on his later style. The young Churchill, in his leap to self-education, must have been the most unusual cavalry subaltern in any European army.

Yet cavalryman he remained at heart, at least at that stage of his life. He seems to have recognized that to serve in the army but not to have smelt powder or wielded cold steel would count against him in the later career of statesmanship for which he yearned. He wanted to fight; he also wanted, with his keen understanding of how easily gallant deeds were lost to sight without publicity, to write his own record of his soldierly exploits. He was shortly to get the chance to achieve both ambitions.

Home on leave in England in May 1897, he learned of the outbreak of fighting on the North-West Frontier of India. He telegraphed at once to General Sir Bindon Blood, who had been appointed to command a punitive expedition, reminding him of a promise made the previous year to take Winston with him if ordered on active service. Without waiting for an answer, he took ship back to India at once and at Bombay found Blood's answer. 'No vacancies. Come as correspondent. Will try to fit you in. B.B.' Winston detoured briefly to Bangalore to get his commanding officer's permission to join the expedition and set out. While his mother lobbied editors in England to secure him accreditation, he managed to get himself appointed by the Allahabad *Pioneer*, Kipling's old newspaper, to the Malakand Field Force. He was to send three hundred words a day. Meanwhile Jennie had persuaded the *Daily Telegraph* to accept dispatches from him at five pounds a column.

On September 17, 1897, Winston fought his first action. A brigade of the Malakand Field Force, pushing into tribal territory, was surprised by the enemy, suffered heavy casualties, and extricated itself with difficulty. The pattern was familiar to any soldier, British or Indian, with experience of frontier warfare. The mountainous Frontier province was British-Indian territory but its border too difficult, both topographically and politically, to administer. Its frontiersmen, Muslim Pathans of fierce warrior habits, resented British attempts to police their fractious lives and, as their tribal areas extended into neighbouring and independent Afghanistan, were always able to take refuge there, summon reinforcements from it, or occasionally use it as a base for deep raids into British India proper as circumstances dictated. The frontiersmen were warriors in the Homeric sense, enjoying fighting for its own sake, often against one another, for the blood feud was central to their way of life. Acutely sensitive to slight, jealous of personal honour, and savagely cruel to an opponent unable any longer to defend himself, they tortured, mutilated, and killed without compunction. They were feared but also admired by the British, who enlisted them as irregular constabulary and even as regular soldiers of the Indian army, always in the knowledge that such brothers-in-arms, once back in tribal territory, would, when the mood took them, snipe at, knife, or castrate sepoys or Tommies as if they were their lifelong enemies.

The Pathans' British and Indian army antagonists were also members of a warrior society, though discipline and hierarchy concealed the similarities. The Malakand Field Force was composed of the two separate elements of the Government of India's military establishment. Some of its units were British regiments, serving a statutory seven-year posting to India. Their soldiers were Kipling's Tommy Atkinses, 'single men in barracks' recruited from the slums, hard drinking, hard living, rejected as a match in marriage by respectable families, but officered by the upper middle class, in the cavalry often by the upper class, to which Winston himself belonged. The British officers of the viceroy's Indian army were also middle class, while their sepoys were drawn from the military castes of the Empire – Rajputs, Sikhs, Punjabi Mussulmans. The darlings of their officers, the high-caste sepoys held the mass of India's millions in disdain; in turn, however, British regiments would not accept Indians as equals. Always in the background was the memory of the Great Mutiny of 1857, when sepoys had murdered European men and women also; there was also the implication that sepoys might break when British soldiers would stand. The British third of India's military establishment existed, unspokenly, to prevent another mutiny, but also to stiffen the bearing of the Indian two thirds on the battlefield.

Sepoys could and would, despite British reservations, fight with ferocity and hold with tenacity. In the Malakand expedition, however, stereotypes were confirmed. While British troops held firm, sepoys ran. Winston was with sepoys who broke, and he was rescued by Tommies who marched forward against fire. The episode may have formed his lifelong belief in the right of the British to rule India.

September 17 began for Winston when he joined the 35th Sikhs on the advance up the Mamund Valley, a Pathan stronghold. At first he rode the grey (white) charger he had bought at the sale of the effects of an officer killed earlier in the campaign. As the firing grew he dismounted and joined a Sikh company that was pushing toward a Pathan village. The village was taken, and the Sikhs halted. Suddenly young Churchill realized that he, four other British officers, and about eighty Sikhs were on their own. They had advanced far ahead of the column, were overlooked from high ground, and, as the heights began to puff with the smoke of aimed rifle fire, were dangerously outnumbered. The Pathans plunged down the hillsides to positions only a hundred yards from the Sikh cluster. Winston took a Lee-Enfield rifle from a sepoy and fired all the ammunition he was handed until the Sikhs' British adjutant panted up to order a retreat. In the withdrawal the adjutant was wounded and, when Winston turned back to rescue him, was killed by a Pathan front-runner. The Sikhs were now in full flight, abandoning their wounded, even though the first rule of frontier warfare was not to leave casualties to the mercy of the enemy. Only at the bottom of the slope was it possible to reorder the ranks. As the Sikhs turned to fire volleys into the dense Pathan masses, the 35th's commanding officer ordered Winston, who still had his grey horse, to gallop off and summon the Buffs – the East Kent Regiment, 3rd of Foot, one of the oldest and most famous British infantry regiments – to their rescue. He had turned away when the spectre of his lone survival, and all the odium that would be his, confronted him. 'I must have the order in writing,' he blurted out. While the colonel struggled with pencil and paper, the notes of a bugle signalling the charge sounded out. 'Here, praise be to God, were the Buffs.'

The Buffs steadied the Sikhs and helped them to recover the ground lost. All the Sikhs' wounded, however, had been killed and mutilated. As the survivors fell back once more, the Pathans followed; the British and Indians succeeded in disengaging only because 'the Buffs were steady as rocks.' Winston does not articulate, in his pell-mell account of the action, the idea that the white man is the brown's superior. It is implicit, however, in what he wrote. Kipling, who loved Indians, thought the same. Had Winston, one wonders, read Kipling's tale *His Chance in Life*, the story of how a Goanese telegraph clerk confronts an Indian mob at his telegraph station and restores civil order? Michele d'Cruze, blue with fear, remembers his trace of white blood and stares rebellion out of his racial inferiors. Kipling's nuances would not have engaged Churchill's interest. His authorial instinct was for the large effect, not for literary subtlety. It is indicative, however, of the ethos of Empire which both embraced that the two took for granted the right of the Briton to rule.

The Empire was once again expanding in the 1890s, following the electoral defeat of the anti-imperialist Gladstone. Britain's possessions and protectorates in West Africa were spreading inland – Winston had written to Jennie of the reputation to be made there by a dashing soldier – but the nation's focus of attention lay on the other side of the continent, in the Sudan, where General Sir Herbert Kitchener was leading a military expedition from Egypt to reestablish British authority on the Upper Nile and avenge the murder of General Charles Gordon. In 1885 Gordon, a deeply devout evangelical Christian but also a standard-bearer of the imperial idea, had been killed in the residency at Khartoum, capital of the Egyptian dependency of the Sudan, by soldiers of the Mahdi, a charismatic Muslim fundamentalist. A relief expedition had been defeated en route to save him, and the disgrace had rankled. Gordon was a hero at home both to the Empire-minded and to his fellow believers, who regarded him as a Christian martyr.

There was more to Kitchener's campaign. Egypt was legally part of the Ottoman Empire but, since 1882, had been ruled by a British agent (governor) and sirdar (military commander), who exercised devolved power. Two other European states, however, had interests on the Upper Nile: Italy had established a colony in Somalia, on the Red Sea coast, and was probing inland (disastrously into Ethiopia in

1896); France, from its huge enclave in Algeria, had already created a Saharan empire and was pushing eastward. There loomed the danger that Britain's de facto Egyptian empire might be cut off from the colonies – in Uganda, Zanzibar, and Kenya – it had already created in East Africa, which it was its ambition to dominate. The outline of a corridor from 'Cairo to the Cape [of Good Hope]' was already forming in the minds of British imperialists. The mission of Kitchener, as sirdar, was therefore not only to avenge Gordon and secure the southern frontier of Egypt against Sudanese incursions, but also to extend the British Empire southward toward its colonies on the Indian Ocean.

To get to Egypt, however, Churchill needed Kitchener's approval, and the great man did not approve of the young subaltern. He shared Winston's brother subalterns' opinion of him as a 'medal-hunter' and 'self-advertiser', 'super-precocious', even 'insufferably bumptious', which he undoubtedly was. Worse, in the sirdar's eyes, he wrote of his senior officers' conduct of operations as if he were a general himself. His newspaper articles were presumptuous. His book *The Story of the Malakand Field Force*, which had appeared in March 1898, was intolerable. In fact, Winston's first full-length literary effort was the success he hoped it to be. He had laid aside another – later to appear as the novel *Savrola* in 1900 – in order to catch the public interest while still hot, and was delighted by both its sales and the opinions it earned. The Prince of Wales, the future Edward VII, had written to praise it: 'Everybody is reading it.' He had also advised Winston, however, 'to stick to the Army before adding MP to your name.' It was a shrewd perception of what Churchill was up to, and sage counsel. Bumptious subalterns do not get on. But even the warnings of the heir to the throne could not deter Winston when he had the bit between his teeth. He knew Egypt was now the place to be and pestered in every direction to get there. Eventually he had an unsolicited stroke of luck. The Prime Minister, Lord Salisbury, had read *The Story of the Malakand Field Force* and admired it. He asked Winston to see him, asked if he could do anything for him, and – told emphatically that there was – wrote on his behalf to the British agent in Cairo. Winston had concurrently a second stroke of luck. An officer of the 21st Lancers, one of Kitchener's British regiments, had just died. The agent, Lord Cromer (Evelyn Baring), proposed Winston in his place. Kitchener was too busy to object. Hopping on a ferry, and not bothering to trouble his commanding officer in distant South India for leave, Winston turned up in the Abbasya barracks in Cairo on August 2, 1898, and joined the 21st's A Squadron. He was fully outfitted, had bought a horse, and was, most important of all, equipped with a commission from the *Morning Post* to send dispatches at £15 a time.

Winston's exploits with the 21st Lancers were to become part of his legend. After a long approach, first by Nile steamer, later across the desert, Winston arrived in late August at Omdurman, only three miles from Khartoum. On September 1 Kitchener's army saw that of the Khalifa, the Mahdi's successor, drawn up in a line of battle across a front of five miles. There was a day's pause, during which Churchill was sent to take a report to Kitchener, who did not acknowledge him, but he was given lunch by the sirdar's chief of staff. Next morning the Khalifa's forty thousand men advanced to attack Kitchener's twenty-six thousand, half British soldiers, half disciplined Egyptians. The following morning the dervishes threw themselves against the British line in a religious fervour. They met the fire of massed artillery, of twenty machine guns, and of thousands of magazine rifles. They fell in swaths. By nine o'clock in the morning the battle was won. Kitchener, however, feared that the dervishes might retreat into the streets of Khartoum and rob him of an easy victory. He therefore decided to order up his British cavalry and sweep the field of the remnants of the enemy before they had the chance to re-form. His order went to the 21st Lancers. At 8.40 a.m. it formed front, 310 strong, trotted forward, and then charged headlong into a mass of three thousand dervishes.

The ground between the lancers and the enemy looked flat. Unperceived, however, there intervened a dry watercourse, 'a *nullah* with steep sloping sides 6 feet deep – 20 feet broad,' as Winston later wrote to Colonel Ian Hamilton. The regiment approached it at the gallop but slowed as it reached the lip. Winston's troop got across without difficulty and struck the dervishes fast. 'Opposite they were 4 deep,' he reported to Jennie later, but the lancers got through into open desert filled with fugitives. Some fired back. Winston, who used his Mauser pistol instead of his sword, believed he had killed '3 for certain – 2 doubtful – one very doubtful.' Finding himself far ahead of his soldiers, he turned back. He was fired at from close range as he retired, but both bullets missed. The regiment had not been so lucky. Twenty-one lancers had been killed, forty-nine wounded, while more than a third of the horses had been hit. The dervishes were devastated. Though the Khalifa tried to organize a second line of resistance at the gates of Khartoum, those of his followers who had escaped the battlefield simply melted into the hinterland. The wounded left on the ground were killed by the victors.

The Nile campaign terminated generally in indignity. The tomb of the Mahdi was desecrated, his body disinterred, and the corpse decapitated, the head being plunged in kerosene and forwarded in a can to Cairo. Strategically, nevertheless, it had been a complete success. The French advance to the Nile was discontinued in the aftermath, and the government of the Sudan was established on the basis of an Anglo-Egyptian condominium, effectively run by British officials whose evident admiration of the Sudanese was warmly returned. The Sudan Political Service and the Sudan Defence Force attracted, between 1898 and 1956, the best of Britain's overseas civil and military servants, making the Sudan a jewel of the Empire.

The termination of the conquest, however, also terminated Winston's interest in Egypt and Sudan. The problem was solved; he sought to move on. After helping the regiment win the Indian polo championship during a brief return visit to the subcontinent in February, he had resigned from the army and sailed for England. He was free to write as he chose. While his campaign experience would provide the material for a second narrative of military action, *The River War*, which was to prove as commercially successful as the first had been, his mind was already on other things, including love and politics. While writing *The River War* in London, at breakneck speed, he had re-encountered a girl he first met in India, Pamela Plowden, whose father was British resident at the court of the nizam of Hyderabad. He had fallen in love. Pamela was beautiful and intelligent, and Winston pressed his suit hard. The truth was, however, that he lacked the touch with women. He himself recognized that he did not understand the opposite sex. He had no romantic guile, expecting that what interested him would also interest a pretty dinner companion. As what interested him was politics, it is not surprising that Pamela did not return his affection. She was sharp enough to see, and to tell him, that his protestations of devotion, though perfectly sincere, disguised his real commitment to Parliament and to power. He was, during his pursuit of her, adopted as Conservative candidate for the Lancashire cotton town of Oldham. She declined to help him with his campaign during July 1899. Though he made a good showing, he lost. Working-class Oldham did not want a Conservative. Pamela, over the course of the next year, decided she did not want Winston. In 1901 she accepted another offer and became Lady Lytton.

In the interim events had whirled Winston away into one of the most dramatic episodes of his life. In October 1899 a long-brewing dispute between the British government and the Boers of South Africa had culminated in the outbreak of war. On October 14, Churchill sailed for the Cape as correspondent for the *Morning Post* at a salary of £250 a month. He had rightly identified that the Boer-British quarrel was certain to be a crisis of Empire and had already prepared his move. Three days before his ship left Southampton, a Boer ultimatum had run out.

It was a bold move by the two small Afrikaner republics to demand that the British Empire dismantle its military apparatus threatening their borders. *Oom* (Uncle) Paul Kruger, the Transvaal president, had decided to take the risk all the same, and his commandos invaded British Natal on October 12 and the other British South African colonies soon afterwards. The quarrel between the Boers and the British was of long standing. Britain had settled Natal in the 1820s but inherited the old Dutch colony of the Cape during the Napoleonic Wars. Its Dutch settlers, who had been making their own way of life since the seventeenth century, objected to British colonial control and, in the Great Trek of 1835–37, migrated northward to found independent farming states. Warlike, legalistic, and fiercely Calvinist, the Boers fought to justify their separateness from the British and their African neighbours alike in a succession of wars – against the Zulus in 1838, against the British in 1881. Had farming been all that was at issue, they might thereafter have subsisted in peace. By the 1890s, however, it had become apparent that the territory of the Transvaal contained some of the richest gold and diamond fields in the world. Johannesburg became a magnet to English-speaking fortune hunters who were soon not only rich but politically demanding. Though 'outlanders', as the Boers called them, they wanted votes and a voice in the Transvaal's government. Confronted by the threat of being outnumbered, the Boers fixed the franchise. In 1896 the outlanders staged a rebellion that failed. In 1899 the Boers made the mistake of carrying the conflict to the enemy. Once they had invaded Britain's South African territory, war was a certainty. Certain, too, seemed the Boers' defeat.

At the outset, and for months afterwards, however, the Boers proved better than the British on the ground. Born to the saddle, and brilliant shots from it, they defeated Tommy Atkins whenever he was met. They also showed themselves to be masters of musketry – with the modern magazine rifle – from entrenched positions. Very soon the British found themselves besieged at Mafeking, Kimberley, and Ladysmith, by Boers who handled both modern rifles and Krupp artillery with skill. In late November and December 1899, the British were to suffer humiliating defeats by Boers entrenched on the banks of the Modder and Tugela Rivers. Worse was to follow, in the Battles of Colenso and Spion Kop. Not until the spring of 1900 would the might of British numbers begin to turn the tide.

At the nadir of British fortunes, during the siege of Ladysmith, young Winston was caught up in a setback typical of those the Boers were frequently inflicting on the British at the time. Only just arrived in South Africa, he found a train that was going from Durban, on the Natal coast, to Estcourt, just short of Ladysmith, then under Boer threat. Scenting the chance to beat his newspaper rivals, he joined the train and started up the line. On the way up-country, he met several army friends, including Reggie Barnes, his companion on the Cuba jaunt. Barnes had been wounded in one of the early battles and uttered a warning. 'You will be told,' he said, that 'the Boers only want one good thrashing to satisfy them. Don't you believe it. They mean going through with this to the end.' Winston took the message to heart. Its truth would form his attitude to popular wars for the rest of his life.

Winston's train was armoured. An anticipation of the tank, the armoured train was in practice an aberration, unable to operate off the fixed line of a railway and vulnerable to any dislocation of the track. On November 15, 1899, Winston's train, nosing forward to Ladysmith, which had just come under siege, was ambushed by a Boer commando, and derailed. He made a spirited effort to separate the damaged from the intact trucks and get the locomotive moving again, in the direction of safety. Enemy fire, however, was too hot – five hundred Boers lined the embankment – and the British were quickly forced to surrender. Winston was among the prisoners. They were marched off under escort and soon incarcerated in an improvised prison camp, the State Model School in Pretoria, capital of the Transvaal.

The Model School, built as a college to train teachers, stands to this day, in the center of Pretoria, a dull red-brick building characteristic of turn-of-the-century architecture all over South Africa. Its conversion into a prisoner-of-war camp entailed the construction around it of a corrugated iron wall on which searchlights played during the hours of darkness. Churchill hated every minute he spent inside. Imprisonment reminded him of his schooldays. 'I certainly hated every minute of my imprisonment more than I have ever hated any other period of my whole life.'

He began to plan escape as soon as he was locked up; fellow prisoners joined the plot. The Boer commandant-general Piet Joubert had already decided that, as a journalist, Churchill should be released. Before that word came through, however, the conspirators made their attempt. His companions, deterred by the activities of the guards, turned back. Winston persisted, hopped over the wall into darkness, and disappeared into the night. He wandered for some hours, hoping to meet a friendly black, until he stumbled on a railwayman's house. The occupant was not Boer but British. As the two men established their identities, Winston asked for help to escape. 'We are all British here,' was the answer, 'and we will see you through.' Winston was hidden at the bottom of a mine shaft for three days, then put into a rail truck loaded with wool going east into Portuguese Mozambique. Through the lies and distractions of other quickly made friends. Winston survived several train inspections to arrive undetected at Lourenço Marques (now Maputo). He took ship there and, on December 23, reached Durban in British South Africa.

His escape had made him famous throughout the Empire, and he was received by jubilant crowds. He might have returned to the press corps crowned with laurels. His instinct, instead, was for action. Brought to see General Sir Redvers Buller, he asked for an officer's commission. His request put Buller in a quandary. As a result of the young Churchill's behaviour on the Frontier as in the Sudan, the War Office had ordered that no officer could act as a war correspondent or vice versa. Buller, however, was short of good officers and recognized Winston to be one. After some agitated reflection, he announced that Churchill could join the South African Light Horse, a wartime creation, as assistant adjutant, without pay. As he was already earning twelve times a subaltern's salary by writing for the *Morning Post*, Winston accepted immediately, donned khaki, stuck the regiment's feather in his hat, and departed for the front.

He was shortly to see all the fighting he sought, first at Spion Kop, a bloody British defeat on the road to besieged Ladysmith; at two smaller battles; then at the relief of Ladysmith on February 28, 1900; and finally at a succession of actions during the advance of British commander in chief Lord Roberts (Frederick Sleigh Roberts) across the Transvaal. He rode unrecognized through Johannesburg before its fall and had the satisfaction of entering Pretoria with the conquering army and helping to release the British prisoners in the State Model School where he had been locked up the previous year. He had nearly been killed in a skirmish at Dewetsdorp, before Johannesburg, when he lost his horse and was rescued by a trooper riding another that bled to death at full gallop with the two men up, and he survived a second armoured train ambush after his departure from Pretoria for Cape Town. Winston took charge of the train's troops under shellfire and was glad to get away unscathed. 'I thought for many years,' he wrote in 1930, 'that the 2-inch Creusot shell which had burst so near us on the embankment was the last projectile I should ever see fired in anger.' He would, in truth, not be in danger of his life again until he commanded the 6th Royal Scots Fusiliers in France in 1915–16. As a soldier, between 1895 and 1900, he had, however, led a charmed life and could count himself lucky to leave South Africa on July 7 untouched by shot or shell, to take up the life of politics in England. His authorship – *London to Ladysmith via Pretoria*, his fourth book, was as successful as the previous three – had made him financially independent, for a time at least, and his profitable journalism had also made him famous. The House of Commons beckoned. He would soon be there.

Yet though politics was to consume Churchill's later youth, adulthood, and maturity, his military years must be counted among the most significant of his life. He never had reason to doubt thereafter his physical courage. He had been shot at many times, often from close range, had fired back with his personal weapons, and had killed other human beings. Winston had seen what death meant with his own eyes, and – though the excitement of making war would possess him throughout both world conflicts – he never lost sight of its tragedy. At a battle on the Tugela River, outside Ladysmith, he came across the dead of the Boer and British armies lying almost side by side, a distinguished-looking Boer burgher of about sixty, a Boer boy scarcely old enough to hold a rifle, 'our own two poor riflemen with their heads smashed like eggshells.' The spectacle touched him to the quick. 'Ah, horrible war, amazing medley of the glorious and squalid, the pitiful and sublime, if modern men of light and leading saw your face closer, simple folk would see it hardly ever.' Churchill did not belong to the world of simple folk, but – even as one of the twentieth century's leading men – he would always strive, in his struggle against the seduction of war's glory, to keep its horror clear before his eyes.

4 Parliament, 1900-1910

THE SOUTH AFRICAN War had almost two years to run when Churchill quit Cape Town for home on July 7, 1900. He shared, however, the belief of most in Britain that, with the occupation of the Transvaal, heartland of Boer nationalism, the back of Afrikaner resistance had been broken. He could not foresee that the Boer intransigents, his future friend Jan Smuts foremost among them, would prolong resistance throughout 1901 and half of 1902. In the process these 'bitter-enders' would introduce the Western world to the concept of guerrilla warfare, of which Churchill would become a passionate exponent in the struggle against Hitler during the Second World War.

He had emphatically played his part in the formal stage of the Boer War. It was with a clear conscience, therefore, that he could resume his search for a seat in Parliament, now the focus of his ambition. The ambition had possessed him, of course, since the death of his father, and perhaps earlier, but had been unachievable without reputation or money. His military exploits had won him a reputation; by his escape from Boer captivity he had made himself one of the best-known young men in Britain. That story had also made money more accessible. People wanted to read his journalism and his latest book, *London to Ladysmith via Pretoria*. They also wanted to hear him in person. Between October 1900 and February 1901 he conducted a relentless lecturing tour in Britain, Canada, and the United States, sometimes earning more than a thousand dollars per lecture, and eventually amassing ten thousand pounds, a huge sum at a time when the most senior civil servant in Britain was paid only one thousand pounds a year. His hard-earned nest egg allowed him to surrender his entitlement to five hundred pounds a year from his mother, his only regular income since leaving the army.

It was also sufficient to support him in public life for several years, as long as he remained single, and it came just in time; for Oldham, which had adopted him as a Conservative candidate in 1899, in a by-election he lost, did so again for the general election of 1900.

That October he was elected by a narrow margin, and he took his seat in the House of Commons on February 14, 1901. The election came to be known as the 'Khaki Election', since it was patriotic enthusiasm for the Boer War from which the Conservatives benefited and the Liberals, characterized as the anti-war party, suffered. Churchill was certainly not antiwar. He made, nevertheless, a curious Conservative. There was a strong element of the 'pro-Boer', the label that damned the Liberals, in his outlook, and he had a Liberal suspicion of high state expenditure for military purposes. In South Africa he had formed a powerful admiration for the Boer citizen-soldiers. His keen understanding of military realities had also brought him to doubt the wisdom of

British efforts to emulate Germany and France in the expansion of the army. He expressed the first sentiment in his maiden speech of February 18, widely hailed as the most brilliant by any new member of recent times, in which he called for a generous peace to be made with the Boers 'fighting in the field', adding, to roars of disapproval, 'and if I were a Boer I hope I should be fighting in the field.'

He raised the second point in a series of subsequent speeches outside and within the House. St John Brodrick, the secretary of state for war, was introducing measures to increase military spending by 15 per cent. The money would go to create three army corps. Why so many, Churchill demanded? One was 'quite enough to fight savages, and three not enough even to begin to fight Europeans.' It was a penetrating point. France and Germany, the latter with the largest army in Europe and already beginning to build a 'high seas' navy, each had more than twenty army corps. A three-corps British army would be eaten up by either. The process, moreover, would be horrible. Drawing on his experience of war fought with modern weapons in South Africa, Churchill warned that 'a European war cannot be anything but a cruel, heartrending struggle, which, if we are ever to enjoy the fruits of victory, must demand, perhaps for several years, the whole manhood of the nation, the entire suspension of peaceful industries, and the concentration to one end of every vital energy of the community.' What, Churchill asked, was the rational alternative to attempting to match the continental countries' military might? It was, he insisted, to concentrate expenditure on the Royal Navy as the instrument that protected Britain's true source of standing in the world, its industrial and commercial strength. 'Why should we sacrifice a game in which we are sure to win, to play a game we are bound to lose? The whole course of our history, the geography of our country, all the evidences of the present situation proclaim beyond doubt that Britain's power and prosperity depend upon the economic command of markets and the Navy's command of the seas.' Addressing a different set of arguments, he went on to appeal to parliamentary and public opinion on an ethical level. 'We shall make a fatal bargain if we allow the moral force which this country has so long exerted to become diminished, or perhaps destroyed, for the sake of the costly, trumpery, military playthings on which the Secretary of State for War has set his heart.'

Churchill's speeches on the Army Estimates of 1901 were remarkable for three reasons. The first is that they reveal an extraordinary prescience. His forecast of the nature of a future great European war, based entirely upon his observation of the effect of high-velocity rifle and high-explosive artillery fire in South Africa, was acutely accurate. What he predicted – heavy casualties and protracted battles – was exactly what came about in France and Belgium from 1914 onward. The second is that they disclose an early and unremarked understanding of the importance of maintaining the nation's prosperity as a positive social good. There are several explanations for that. Oldham was a working-class constituency, and Churchill recognized the claims of labour to security of employment and a decent wage. His own father's commitment to 'Tory democracy' had been transmitted to him. He was, at the time if not always in the future, a believer in free trade as a means to securing high living standards for all. The third remarkable dimension of this early speech is the commitment it reveals to Britain's moral particularism. In his great wartime speeches of 1940-45, Churchill was to proclaim time and again his belief that his country was superior – by reason of its championship of democracy, personal liberty, and the rule of law – to the totalitarian regimes it opposed. Though cynics might try to identify an expediency of the moment, his speeches of 1901 demonstrate a consistent stance. Churchill believed, with fundamental force, in his country's moral elevation above others, by reason of its electoral form of government and legal guarantees of the freedom of the individual.

His opposition to increased expenditure on the army might have been judged a single-issue point of difference between himself and his father's Conservative Party. Soon, however, he was to drift further away. Lord Randolph's concern to resurrect his party's Disraelian appeal to the working man, 'Tory democracy', loomed ever larger in his outlook. In December 1901 he began to read a book by the social reformer Seebohm Rowntree on the condition of the respectable working class. *Poverty: A Study of Town Life* was based on a survey of social conditions in York, not far from his own Lancashire constituency of Oldham. It revealed that a quarter of the city's population lived in a poverty that killed a high proportion of the newborn and stunted the growth of the survivors. On the pretext of deploring the consequences for recruitment to the armed forces, Churchill made *Poverty* a text of his speeches and writings. 'It is quite evident,' he wrote in December 1901 to a senior Conservative official,

that the American labourer is a stronger, larger, healthier, better fed, and consequently more efficient animal than a large proportion of our population, and this surely a fact which our unbridled Imperialists, who have no thought but to pile up armaments, taxation and territory, should not lose sight of. For my own part, I see little glory in an Empire which can rule the waves and is unable to flush its own sewers.

This was Radical talk. Churchill was already identified as a Tory radical, and soon he would cease to be a Tory altogether. Early in his parliamentary career he began to associate with members of the Liberal opposition, then to make common cause with a dozen fellow Tories, led by Lord Hugh Cecil and known as the 'Hughligans', or 'Hooligans', who dissociated themselves from their party's plutocracy. They wanted a party readier to accept social responsibility, less devoted to the moneyed cause. Churchill's particular concerns were with generosity to the defeated Boers, reduced military spending, and maintenance of free trade. The Tories were traditionally the landed party, but the success of Liberal economic policy in the years of Britain's dominance of world commerce had weakened their solicitude for farmers and estate owners. With the rise of American and German economic power, pushing Britain from first to third place among the world's manufacturing nations, all producers in the country, including agricultural producers, began to demand a return to protective taxes – tariffs – on foreign imports.

In 1902 the government introduced a proposal to tax foreign grain. By 1903 Joseph Chamberlain, a former Radical who had become a Tory stalwart, was advocating a general programme of tariffs, with exceptions for imports from the Empire – 'imperial preference'. Churchill opposed both consistently and loudly, in a series of speeches delivered throughout the country. In May 1903 he announced that commitment to tariffs would cause the disappearance of the 'old Conservative Party with its religious convictions and constitutional principles.' In its place, 'a new party will arise, rich, materialistic and secular, whose opinions will turn on tariffs and whose lobbies will be crowded with the touts of protected industries.' Churchill and his friends began to vote against the government and to talk of the formation of an alternative party, committed to the best of the Tory and Liberal policies (shades of his father's so-called Fourth Party). Arthur Balfour, the Prime Minister, tried to diffuse the rising divisions within Conservatism by simultaneously accepting Chamberlain's resignation and dismissing his three leading free trade ministers. It did no good. Protection versus free trade had become a central issue of politics that would split his party if it was not settled by vote at a general election. Churchill warned of the consequences of winning an election under the protectionist banner. On May 13, 1904, speaking to a Liberal audience in Manchester, the city that was home to the free trade cause, he foresaw a 'party of great vested interests, banded together in a formidable federation: corruption at home, aggression to cover it up abroad; the trickery of tariff juggles, the tyranny of a party machine; sentiment by the bucketful, patriotism by the imperial pint … dear food for the million, cheap labour for the millionaire.'

Churchill was overstating his case. Chamberlain was possessed by genuine concern for the survival of British industry in the face of more efficient foreign competitors, which profited by the earliness of Britain's Industrial Revolution to imitate and better it; Balfour was a high-minded intellectual whom no one accused of corruption or lobbyism. Winston's convictions were, nevertheless, heartfelt. While he wanted to be a Conservative, it was on his father's terms of Tory democracy, which valued the needs of the working man as high as those of his employer and landlord. By early 1904 Churchill's separation from his party was almost complete. The government front bench walked out on him when he demanded that the Prime Minister should declare his position on protection. His own constituency association in Oldham recorded its loss of confidence in him. On May 31, 1904, he entered the House, bowed to the speaker, and turned to sit on the Liberal benches, in the seat his father had occupied when the Conservatives were in opposition to Gladstone's Liberal government.

He had 'crossed the floor'. Crossing the floor, leaving one party to join another, is the riskiest move a British parliamentarian can make. In so doing he forfeits all former political friendship, without any guarantee that he will find affection among his new fellows. It was fortunate for Churchill that a general election loomed, offering the chance of a fresh start in a new constituency. As a committed free trader he had already made his mark in Manchester, the free trade city par excellence, and he was now adopted by Manchester North West. His opposition to the Conservatives' Aliens Bill, intended to stem the influx of Jewish refugees from Russian pogroms, recommended him to the electors, many of whom were Jews working in the clothing trade; among all Churchill's prejudices, anti-Semitism was not one. He already had many Jewish friends and was soon to become a Zionist.

At the general election of January 1906, Churchill won his seat by a comfortable majority. His victory was a small element in a Liberal triumph, which returned 377 Liberals to the House of Commons but only 157 Conservatives; the Irish Parliamentary Party won 83 seats, a figure it had consistently achieved for a generation; the new Labour Party, on whose support the Liberals could count, 53. The Irish members, too, generally supported the Liberals on every issue except that of denial of Home Rule. Churchill, still a Unionist – the Unionists opposed Irish home rule – as his father had been, had compromised his principles by agreeing to a limited measure of Irish self-government. What he was prepared to accept fell far short of what the Irish nationalists demanded and what the Liberal leadership was prepared to concede. A real Irish crisis still, however, lay in the future.

In 1910 Churchill was to be offered by Herbert Asquith, the new Liberal Prime Minister, the Chief Secretaryship of Ireland, the ministerial post devoted to Irish affairs. It is fascinating to speculate what he might have made of it. Direct engagement with the leaders of the Irish national movement might have mobilized all his political ingenuity in the achievement of a settlement of their demands, which were moderate enough: domestic self-government within the United Kingdom. In the event, Churchill refused Asquith's offer, though for personal rather than political reasons. He hoped for higher things, which he was to get; he seems to have recognized also that his Unionism was too deep-seated to allow him to concede the liberties the Irish Parliamentary Party sensed it was upon the point of securing.

In 1910 Churchill was President of the Board of Trade, a position he had held since 1908, when he had been promoted to that office from the under-secretaryship for the colonies. At the Colonial Office he had had the satisfaction of granting self-government to both the Transvaal and the Orange Free State, measures he advocated to the House in words that anticipated Woodrow Wilson's policy of securing freedom for 'small nations' in the aftermath of the First World War. 'The cause of the poor and the weak all over the world,' he said, 'will [be] sustained; and everywhere small peoples will get more room to breathe; and everywhere great empires will be encouraged by our example to step forward into the sunshine of a more gentle and more generous age.'

The complexity of Churchill's character and thinking are nowhere better exemplified than in those words. The aspirations of the Catholic Irish were identical to those of the Boers and similar to those of the burgeoning Indian national movement. Against the concept of an independent India Churchill would, however, shut his face, right up to the grant of Indian independence in 1947; Irish nationalism remained repugnant to his Unionist soul until Irish rebellion forced a change of heart in 1921. Then it was the character and courage of Michael Collins, the Sinn Fein guerrilla leader, which altered Churchill's mood. He came to admire Collins, as he had learned to admire the Boer warriors during his struggle against them in 1899–1900. He never came to admire the Indian nationalists, who took their lead from the pacifist Gandhi rather than the revolutionaries in the independence movement. Democrat and institutionalist though he was, Churchill had a gut sympathy for fighters. The Boers were fighters; the Indians were not, nor the Irish either until the extremity of the Anglo-Irish crisis was reached in 1916. Indians he was always to hold in contempt; eventually he was to grant the Irish a grudging respect; it was the fighting Boers who enjoyed his wholehearted admiration.

This *Weltanschauung* was to distort Churchill's conduct of operations seriously during his years of greatness as war leader in 1940–45. In July 1940, the month when Hitler's conquest of Europe became the central fact of strategic reality, Churchill instructed the head of the Special Operations Executive (SOE) to do what the Boers had done in South Africa after 1900 and Sinn Fein in Ireland after 1918: to render alien government impossible by a sustained campaign of guerrilla warfare. The SOE's campaign, by which Churchill set such store, failed almost utterly in the face of the Nazis' brutal repression.

A pre-totalitarian morality ruled, however, in the years when Churchill had to choose between the Chief Secretaryship of Ireland and another post. As President of the Board of Trade he pursued the radical policies espoused when he crossed the floor to become a Liberal. The harsh lot of the working man remained close to his heart. He advocated shorter working hours, ampler educational opportunities, better medical care, the creation of state-run employment agencies for job seekers, provision for state pay during periods of unemployment, and old-age pensions. His successors in the office, David Lloyd George, the Welsh Liberal firebrand, foremost among them, would reap the credit for such legislation; the fulfillment of his programme would only eventually be achieved by the Labour government that defeated him in the general election of 1945. Between 1908 and 1910, however, Churchill spoke, wrote, and acted as a social revolutionary and, had events fallen out otherwise and time been given him, might be so remembered in British political annals.

Instead Churchill was to become an ogre to the Labour

movement after 1910, largely because of measures he had to take for the maintenance of public order during his next ministerial appointment, as Home Secretary, at a time of severe industrial unrest. All that lay in the future, however, during his first Colonial years, which were a happy time, perhaps the happiest of his life. In May 1908 he found a new and secure seat at Dundee, in Scotland; in September he married. He had known his bride, Clementine Hozier, since 1904 and had met her subsequently several times, at balls and house parties. No spark had been struck. At the beginning of April 1908, however, the two were guests together at his mother's house, where Clementine's 'intellectual quality and strong reserves of noble sentiment' – his words in a subsequent letter to her – commanded his attention. The young Winston had been in love several times, but poverty or the call of adventure had brought the affairs to nothing. Now in his early thirties and an established politician, he clearly needed a wife and swiftly decided that Clementine must be she.

No material motive impelled him. Clemmie was poor and, though well born, not from the grand aristocracy. Her mother, Blanche, daughter of an earl, had married a divorced soldier, Colonel Sir Henry Hozier, a difficult, frightening man who later abandoned her also. Lady Blanche had scrimped to give her three daughters a respectable upbringing, living in lodgings and sending Clemmie to an unfashionable day school instead of engaging a governess. That proved an advantage. Clemmie as a result was better educated than her social equals and, though frustrated in her hope to attend a university, learned French well enough to earn a little money by giving lessons. An ordinary schooling also reinforced her natural good sense, making her an unusual being for the time: an upper-class girl with the outlook of a member of the professional middle class. Beatrice Webb, the leading lady Socialist of the age, wrote approvingly of her 'earnestness'.

She wrote also of her charm and prettiness. But merely pretty Clemmie was not: she was strikingly beautiful, with severe features, large eyes, and dark hair. Winston was bowled over by her looks, which she kept to the end of her long life. He had courted other beautiful women before, however, including the famous actress Ethel Barrymore. Looks meant less to him than character. In one of his early letters to her he wrote of his hopes of laying the 'foundations of a frank and clear-eyed friendship which I should certainly value and cherish with many serious feelings of respect.' Respect for her qualities soon pushed his feelings beyond the desire for friendship. They were reciprocated. During the summer of 1908 Clemmie, who was no stranger to strong emotion and had already broken off one engagement to another suitor, began to fall in love with Winston, as he with her. His main thought now was to arrange circumstances in which he could propose. The occasion came when he was able to invite her to Blenheim Palace, his birthplace, in early August. On the morning of August 11, they made a tour of the grounds and stopped at the Temple of Diana. When they emerged, they were engaged. Clemmie had secured his heart.

She kept it all their life together, which was often stormy. 'Shy but passionate' was their daughter Mary Soames's description of her mother's nature. Clemmie made friends with difficulty and was never socially intimate with any man but her husband. Day-to-day married life with Winston was for her nevertheless a trial. His carelessness with money, his gambling instinct, his endless appetite for talk, his ease in company – particularly with friends she correctly identified as the wrong sort – his intellectual curiosity, and his artistic and creative bent all grated. Clemmie was simple where Winston was complex, sensitive where he was forthright. Her strength of character nevertheless matched his, as did her directness when roused. She might have been happier with a more ordinary man, he with someone more conventionally feminine. Theirs, nonetheless, was certainly a marriage of true minds. They loved each other deeply and, whatever their differences, always returned to mutual understanding. Clemmie was a clever as well as a strong woman. Winston would not otherwise have married her.

They were wed at St Margaret's, Westminster, on September 12, 1908. Their first child, Diana, was born the following year; their only son, Randolph, in 1911. Sarah was born in 1914, Mary in 1922; the fourth child, Marigold, lived from 1918 only until 1921. Both parents took enormous pleasure in the company of their children – the daughters especially, before marriage, providing Clemmie with the friendship she found difficult to win elsewhere. Winston was the most affectionate of fathers, though Sarah made the most unsuitable of marriages and Randolph's waywardness would have tried the patience of any parent. Randolph emerged as a sort of caricature of Winston, insufferably bumptious, garrulous, and attention-seeking. He tried to make careers both in politics and journalism, proving an embarrassment at elections and descending to sensationalism in the newspapers. His only redeeming feature was his heartfelt devotion to his father, whose official biographer he much later became. In Mary, a girl of sweet nature and high intelligence, Clemmie and Winston found the consolation of their old age.

In the year after Diana's birth, the course of her father's political career took a new turn. The social policy of the Liberals, of which Churchill as President of the Board of Trade was a standard-bearer, was directed onto a collision course with the country's political and social establishment. Liberal innovations, old-age pensions foremost, would cost money, which David Lloyd George, Asquith's new Chancellor of the Exchequer, proposed to find by increasing the income tax and introducing a supertax on the very rich; he also proposed to raise revenue from alcohol. The House of Lords, the direct target of the supertax, announced its intention to oppose the 1909 budget, the 'People's Budget', and defeated it by 375 votes to 75, thanks to the appearance of numbers of 'backwoods peers' who never normally attended sessions of the Lords. Lloyd George ascribed the defeat to 'five hundred men, chosen accidentally from among the unemployed.' Asquith, however, was not prepared to pass the setback off with a joke. In January 1910 he 'went to the country'. Fierce campaigning by the Conservatives greatly reduced the Liberal majority, emboldening the Lords to threaten sustained resistance. Asquith responded by introducing a Parliament Bill, by which the Lords would be prevented from voting down money bills introduced into the Commons. The issue was one of straight democracy: the right of a democratically elected lower chamber to raise and spend taxes implicitly voted by the mandate of the electorate at large, without interference by a tiny minority of hereditary legislators. When the Lords stood on constitutional principle, Asquith threatened to require King Edward, acting on 'the advice of his ministers', to create sufficient new peers to outnumber the anti-Liberal majority in the upper house. Recognizing that the Prime Minister meant business, the Lords caved in. Although the year's second general election, in December 1910, called to confirm the Parliament Bill, created an exact stalemate between Liberals and Conservatives (or Unionists, as they were then known, because of the Irish issue) of 272 to 272, the weight of forty Labour and eighty Irish votes ensured the Liberals' continuation in power. The Lords would thereafter act only as a 'revising' chamber, allowed to amend ill-drafted bills, not to block the will of the people expressed through the Commons.

Churchill should have been the hero of the Liberals' constitutional victory of 1910. The measures demanding the taxes that made the 1909 budget the 'People's Budget' were largely his: a general unemployment benefit (the 'Winston Churchill'), rather than the sickness benefit alone (the 'Lloyd George'). Somehow it was the sickness benefit – the precursor of the general medical care enshrined in Labour's National Health Service (NHS) of 1948 – that caught popular attention rather than Churchill's employment policies, and Lloyd George who got the credit.

Lloyd George's supplantation of Asquith as Prime Minister at the height of the crisis of the First World War in 1916 owed a great deal to his triumph as the 'People's Chancellor' six years earlier. It was then that he had established himself as a master of debate in the Commons and as a spellbinder of crowds, displaying gifts of oratory that Churchill even at the height of his powers was never to emulate. In 1916, moreover, Churchill's claims to the leadership were compromised by his espousal of flawed strategies – particularly the failed attempt (at great cost in lives) to 'knock Turkey out of the war' by the landings at Gallipoli – that cast doubt on his judgement. Nevertheless, it is clear in retrospect that the more radical social reformer of the two was Churchill, and that, had not the chance of politics drawn his career away into non-social fields, he might have gone on to carry his party even further toward the achievement of universal welfare, which was to be the single most important movement in British domestic affairs for the rest of the century.

5 The Centre of Events, 1910–1915

THE REDIRECTION OF Churchill's political life had begun even before the constitutional crisis of 1910 broke. In February, following the first of that year's two general elections, he had been appointed Home Secretary, responsible for police, penal, and public-order affairs. The need to contain industrial unrest, fomented by the recession of 1909, forced Churchill to deploy the police against strikers on several occasions, particularly against miners in Wales. At one stage he was even obliged to put troops on standby during riots at Tonypandy, an action for which the Labour movement never forgave him. 'Remember Tonypandy!' was a cry that haunted him for years after his return to the Conservative Party in 1925, and helped to make him, quite unfairly, better remembered as a Home Secretary hostile to the working classes than as the President of the Board of Trade who had been their friend.

The single most memorable episode of his time at the Home Office was, however, exotic – an anarchist outrage quite uncharacteristic of staid Edwardian Britain. On January 2, 1911, two Russian anarchists, led by a man known as Peter the Painter, killed three policemen trying to arrest them in the course of a burglary. Next day they were traced to a house in Sydney Street in the East End of London. There they killed another policeman. The police officer in charge summoned twenty Scots Guardsmen, armed with rifles, from the Tower of London just down the road; soon a machine gun was sent for and a troop of Royal Horse Artillery. Churchill was quickly on the spot. 'It was a striking scene in a London street,' he later told Asquith, 'firing from every window, bullets chipping the brickwork, police and Scots Guards armed with loaded weapons.' A photographer caught it: Churchill in top hat and astrakhan collar, Scots Guards in grey overcoats and pipe-clayed belts, an urchin grinning from a lean-to roof above their heads. The picture is a perfect period piece, down to the hanging gaslight, the shoddy shopfronts, and the slimy cobbles in the street. What it does not show, for Churchill's expression is indistinct, is that he was in his element. The smell of powder, the scent of danger, must have brought back his youth. He did not, as was later alleged, take charge, but it may be guessed that he would have done so had the siege been protracted. As things turned out, the house caught fire, the shooting ceased, and, when the conflagration died down, the bodies of two of the terrorists were found within. Of Peter the Painter there was no trace, a perfect conclusion to the Joseph Conradian quality of the Sydney Street siege. It was to be described in every life of Churchill later written.

Peter the Painter was a figure of his time, a manifestation of the belief in danger from within afflicting all contemporary governments, but particularly the Eastern empires, Austria-Hungary and Russia, with their kaleidoscopes of discontented nationalities. What it threatened was not a real menace to the authority of states, which were all strong enough to suppress rebellion and contain terrorism whenever either appeared. It was a symptom of the psychic instability of the multi-national monarchies, which mistrusted their own peoples and feared that minorities straddling international frontiers would provoke crises bringing on general war. In this climate of insecurity European states had, in the forty years before 1910, continuously enlarged their armed forces as a precaution against imagined danger.

Germany had done more. Committed to making itself the dominant military state in an uneasy continental Europe, it also chose after 1900 to make itself an oceanic match for island Britain. It was an ill-judged move. Before 1900 Britain had no quarrel with the German empire. Once Germany announced its intention to create a high-seas fleet of first-class battleships, Britain and its Royal Navy were put on their mettle. The Royal Navy had, in the century since Trafalgar, been the unchallenged mistress of the seas. Behind its wooden, later iron-clad walls, Britain had held itself aloof from foreign alliances. 'Splendid isolation' was the theme of British foreign policy from long before Churchill's birth until his early maturity. The supremacy of its navy ensured that Britain need fight no war it did not choose to enter. It had in fact fought many small wars, almost all dedicated to enlarging its enormous empire, which by 1900 was the largest the world had ever seen. Only in 1854, when it chose to Oppose Russia in the Crimea, had it fought a conventional Great Power continental war. By 1911, when Churchill ceased to be Home Secretary, that conflict was long in the past. His new appointment, as First Lord of the Admiralty, brought him to the forefront of Britain's involvement in the growing European military confrontation.

The transformation of Churchill the social reformer into Churchill the forthright navalist was abrupt and almost total. It was not an unnatural transition, however. Even at the Board of Trade and the Home Office he had sustained his connection with the services, finding opportunities to attend the 'Kaiser manoeuvres' (presciently observing that German soldiers could march thirty-five miles a day, as they were to do on the advance into France in August 1914) and conscientiously attending the summer camps of his volunteer regiment, the Oxfordshire Hussars; there exists a photograph of Major Churchill, wearing the Oxfordshire Hussars uniform, beside the Kaiser at the Imperial manoeuvres of 1909. In 1912 he also began to take flying lessons, believing that aircraft would soon be weapons of war; in his flying life he became competent, survived a crash, but never actually acquired a pilot's licence, though he was to wear pilot's wings later in life. After 1911, however, it was the Royal Navy that consumed his military interests. As a social reformer he had vigorously opposed the battleship-building program provoked by Germany's naval expansion, seeing the cost of dreadnoughts – the new, swift, turbine-engined, heavily armoured, heavily armed battleships that had rendered all predecessors obsolete – as a direct threat to welfare spending; the thinking followed his train of thought developed during his opposition to Brodrick's policy of military expansion during the Boer War. He was later to sum up the course of the dreadnought debate, with characteristic wit, in the words, 'The Conservatives wanted six, the Liberals wanted four; we compromised on eight.'

Once he was responsible for battleship building, Churchill rejected all compromise over numbers. Germany was building dreadnoughts as fast as money allowed. Churchill, now that he was the accountable minister, proved determined to continue outbuilding the Germans. Dreadnoughts, named after the first of the type, were after all a British conception, and he was resolute in his intent that the Royal Navy should maintain its superiority in dreadnought numbers over the German. As First Lord of the Admiralty, however, Churchill took an interest in ensuring Britain's naval supremacy that went much further than budgeting for more battleships. He had a vessel at his disposal, the Admiralty yacht *Enchantress*, and in it he spent more than two hundred days between October 1911 and August 1914, visiting dockyards, anchorages, and outstations of the fleet, to inform himself of the navy's readiness for war and assure its sailors of their political chief's support for their dedication to duty.

He derived essential support during his prewar years in office from the retired Admiral of the Fleet, Sir John Fisher, who, as First Sea Lord, had been professional head of the navy. 'Jackie' Fisher was electric. Not only had he sponsored the supersession of the navy's old ironclads and the introduction of the revolutionary dreadnought; he had also instituted a social revolution within the navy itself, abolishing the distinction between 'seaman' and 'engineer' officers and insisting that, in an age of technology, both should be trained within the same system. Fisher was that rare but valuable bird, a creative eccentric. Brave beyond question, a seadog to his fingertips, he had no truck with the settled order of things and was forever on the search for a better way, a faster ship, a deadlier weapon. He expressed his views in extravagant language, often signing his letters to Churchill 'yours till hell freezes over' or with some other colourful farewell. His nature was as passionate as Churchill's, his mind as quick; it was inevitable that the two should quarrel, but their differences were soon made up. In 1914 Churchill would bring Fisher back to his old office as First Sea Lord. In the interim he did much to guide Churchill's mind and sustain his determination to maintain Britain's 60 per cent superiority in capital ships – battleships and battle cruisers – over Germany.

Churchill could and later did take credit for commissioning the *Queen Elizabeth* class of fast battleships, armed with fifteen-inch guns and propelled by oil, a vastly superior fuel to coal; in order to ensure a certain supply, he also negotiated the purchase of the Anglo-Iranian Oil Company (later British Petroleum [BP]), a very early example of state intervention in industry. He founded the Royal Naval Air Service (RNAS), equipped with aircraft and airships, and coined the term 'seaplane' for its floatplanes. He also insisted on the establishment of a Naval General Staff, in the teeth of seadog opposition. As navies everywhere tended then, and sometimes still now, to do, the Royal Navy esteemed sea time above all other formative experiences in its officers' careers; it feared that specialist staff officers would become blue-uniformed intellectuals, detached from the realities of life aboard ship. Churchill was obliged to dismiss the First Sea Lord, Admiral Sir Arthur Wilson, for his intransigent opposition to the innovation. That was not to be the only change of command he forced. Wilson's successor, Admiral Sir Francis Bridgeman, proved not to be to Churchill's taste and he dismissed him also, appointing Prince Louis of Battenberg, a minor member of the royal family, in his place. Widely regarded as the ablest admiral of his seniority, Prince Louis was removed after the outbreak of war in 1914 because public opinion denounced him as 'German'. His son, later Lord Mountbatten of Burma, made it his life's career to expunge the slur.

The royal family took the keenest interest in naval affairs. George V was truly a sailor king, having served much of his life afloat; his sons, the future kings Edward VIII and George VI, were being educated at the Royal Naval College. Churchill diligently corresponded with the King on naval matters, and there survives a long series of letters on the naming of battleships, a subject dear to both, particularly to Churchill with his love of the striking word. At one stage he was arguing for *Oliver Cromwell* and *Ark Royal*. The King would not have *Oliver Cromwell* at any price and disliked *Ark Royal*, though it had been the name of the flagship in the Spanish Armada battle of 1588. He got his way, though *Ark Royal* would re-emerge as the name of a succession of famous British aircraft carriers. Churchill, however, got *Iron Duke*, in which Admiral Sir John Jellicoe was to fly his flag at the Battle of Jutland in 1916.

Over actual ships, as opposed to ship names, Churchill's real battle was with the Chancellor, Lloyd George, whose anxiety to spend on schools and welfare, the social causes he had shared with Winston during the first Liberal government of the century, was threatened by the enormous costs of naval rearmament. Desperate to outbuild the Germans, Churchill demanded in Cabinet ever larger sums. Almost at the same time, he was attempting to negotiate an agreement with the kaiser to contain the naval race, but to no avail. The German Naval Law of 1912 announced much new construction. Churchill's duty to the defence of the nation's coasts and trade, of its enormous merchant fleet, in which more than half the world's goods were carried, obliged him to press for the money he needed. The two antagonists exchanged notes in Cabinet on July 1, 1914, in the last month of peace. Lloyd George wrote, 'Had there been any other Chancellor of the Exchequer your Naval Bill would have been cut by millions.' Churchill replied, 'There would also have been another First Lord of the Admiralty! And who can say that there would not have been another Government?'

The struggle over military versus civil spending was by then almost academic. On August 4, 1914, Britain was obliged, through its treaty commitment to defend Belgian neutrality, to declare war on Germany, whose soldiers by that day were deep into Belgian territory. At the moment Britain's ultimatum to Germany expired, Churchill issued his first order of the war: COMMENCE HOSTILITIES WITH GERMANY. The fleet was prepared. During July it had conducted a mock mobilization. When it became clear that the Sarajevo crisis was not to be resolved by diplomacy, Winston had ordered the reservists to remain on duty. The navy was therefore at total readiness as peace became war.

There was no immediate clash of battleships. The German High Seas Fleet remained in harbour, awaiting the opportunity for a successful sally into the North Sea. The British Grand Fleet swung at anchor in Scapa Flow, the island roadsteads north of Scotland, where it blocked the exits into the Atlantic the Germans sought. For the moment there was a strategic stalemate, not to be broken until the Germans risked and lost battle at Jutland, two years later. The stalemate was a tribute to the excellence of Churchill's preparations. Those did not, however, preclude naval losses. A U-boat, soon to prove Germany's most potent maritime weapon, sank three old British cruisers off Holland, ships of no worth but crammed with valuable lives; then another U-boat sank one of Britain's newest battleships.

Churchill meanwhile had thrown himself pell-mell into the war on land. As First Lord he commanded the Royal Marines as well as the navy; he also had at his disposal large numbers of sailors surplus to fleet requirements. Out of the two elements he was quickly to form a Royal Naval Division (RND), equipped to fight ashore. The opportunity to use it came soon. While the mass of the German army thrust into northern France, driving the French and the British Expeditionary Force (BEF) before it, the right wing was marching through central Belgium, threatening to overwhelm King Albert I's tiny army. After being forced to abandon Brussels, the King decided to concentrate his forces in the fortress of Antwerp, which guarded the mouth of the Scheldt Estuary. Should the fortress fall, the way would be opened for the Germans to sweep along the Channel coast, capturing the ports that defended the Channel narrows. On September 9, Churchill made an early visit to one, Dunkirk, where an advance element of the RNAS had already been based. He made two more visits in the next fortnight and in the course of his forays came to the conclusion that the key to holding the Channel ports lay in reinforcing Antwerp. By persistent argument he brought the Secretary of State for War, Kitchener, to share his view, and on October 3, eccentrically dressed in the uniform of an Elder Brother of Trinity House, the body that controls Britain's lighthouses, arrived in Antwerp, the marine brigade of the RND following close behind.

The Germans were at the city's gates, the Belgian defenders 'weary and disheartened'. Churchill breathed fire; the Belgian city governor promised to sustain the defence; the Royal Marines were soon in the firing line. On October 6 the Belgians even mounted a counterattack, as the sailor brigades of the RND deployed. Churchill was exultant, but the relief he had organized was short-lived. Eight thousand British sailors and the exhausted Belgians could not hold sixty thousand Germans at bay. On April 9 the governor surrendered the city while the RND escaped in the nick of time along the coast to Dunkirk.

Still, Dunkirk had been saved, and the Antwerp adventure had won sufficient time for the BEF, retracing the course of its retreat after the victory on the Marne, to establish secure positions on the French and Belgian coasts that the Germans were never to breach throughout the war. Churchill's foray had been a success. It had had another effect as well, awakening in him a vision of how amphibious forces could be used to alter the course of operations. Any alteration to the stalemate that, in its aftermath, gripped the Western Front was acutely desirable. Some ingenious British soldiers were already working on the idea of adapting caterpillar tractors as trench-crossing machines. Churchill, who saw the point and coined the term 'land ship' enthusiastically supported them. Their concept, given prototype form as early as December 1915, was to become the tank. Even while it was under development, however, Churchill was thinking of other means to break the deadlock. On December 29, 1914, he wrote to Asquith to demand, rhetorically, 'Are there not other alternatives than sending our armies to chew barbed wire in Flanders?'

The scheme he proposed then was to send the fleet into the Baltic, from which it could transport Russian troops to the German coast to attack Berlin. That was fantasy: huge minefields barred the way. Earlier in the month he had proposed a more promising idea: to attack the Gallipoli Peninsula, which guarded the approaches to the Turkish capital, Constantinople. That was to become the dominant theme of British strategic effort throughout 1915. Turkey, the Ottoman Empire, had throughout the Victorian age been a British client state. Because of poor diplomacy it had then been allowed to become Germany's, and by October 31 it was Britain's enemy. Its armies were directed against Russia, but Churchill saw that, if the narrow passage of the Dardanelles, leading from the Mediterranean to the Black Sea, could be forced and Constantinople taken, Allied supplies could be shipped directly to the Black Sea ports of Russia, thus intensifying the weight of attack it could apply to Germany's eastern front.

The case took considerable arguing. By March, however, the War Council, a new inner cabinet of which Churchill was a member, had accepted it, and on March 18 the attempt began. It was made with a force of old British – and French – battleships, the dreadnoughts being judged too valuable to risk in constricted waters. Had the ships been deployed earlier, the attempt to 'force the narrows' might have worked. Ill-advisedly there had been several half-cocked attacks already: a bombardment of the ports at the entrance immediately after Turkey's entry into the war, two bombardments in February, a marine landing. By March the Turks were ready; they had brought up artillery, they had laid mines. As a result March 18 was a disaster. Three battleships were sunk, three disabled. The fleet turned about and never entered the narrows again. Britain was by then, however, committed, and on April 25 landed troops to seize the shores of the narrows. They included a large number of men from the Australian and New Zealand Army Corps (ANZAC), together with a French contingent; Churchill's RND landed soon after.

Small footholds were secured, but the Turks, commanded by Mustafa Kemal, later Kemal Atatürk, the founder of modern Turkey, counterattacked and hedged the Allies in. Trenches, defended by barbed wire, were dug; artillery was emplaced. Within weeks Gallipoli had become a miniature Western Front, only a few miles square but as impervious to attack as the war zone in France and Belgium. In August a secondary landing was launched. It too was contained. Casualties by then had mounted into the hundreds of thousands; no progress promised; winter was approaching. In November it was decided to evacuate, an operation successfully concluded in January 1916.

The failure of Gallipoli was to haunt Churchill for decades afterward. Even before it was confirmed by evacuation, it had brought about his political downfall. In May, Asquith decided that maintenance of the war effort required his Liberal government to share power with the Conservatives, and a coalition was formed. Part of the price the Conservatives extracted was that Churchill should cease to be First Lord. He had become their bugbear, a floor-crosser who taunted their leading men, vaunted his talents, and was now branded a loser. Churchill pleaded, but in vain. He might have survived had his friend 'until hell freezes over', Fisher, the First Sea Lord, not simultaneously insisted on resigning. Churchill tried to persuade Asquith that he had found a sailor willing to replace the old salt. The Prime Minister replied, 'No, this will not do. I have decided to form a National Government ... and a very much larger reconstruction will be required.'

Churchill's pleadings continued. On May 21 he asked, 'Let me stand or fall by the Dardanelles.' That afternoon he realized that he had fallen. In utter humiliation he told the prime minister, 'I will accept any office – the lowest if you like – that you care to offer me ... until the affairs in which I am deeply concerned [the direction of the war] are settled satisfactorily, as I think they will be.' As a sop Asquith offered him the non-executive post of Chancellor of the Duchy of Lancaster. Since it carried continued membership in the War Council, Churchill took it. He recognized, however, that his enemies had got the better of him, and, as the Gallipoli campaign drew out into defeat, he succumbed slowly into political silence. As a consolation he found a country retreat, where he could enjoy the company of his children and take strength from Clemmie's fierce loyalty. It was during this time that he took up painting; it was to be, as his secretary of many years, Edward Marsh, was to record, 'a distraction and a sedative that brought a measure of ease to his frustrated spirit.'

Such frustration could not last long. Churchill was not only a man of action, he was also a man of honour. He had been a soldier and, while brother officers, including his brother, Jack, were in uniform and at war, his nature rebelled at not sharing their risks. On November 18, 1915, he left his country retreat, Clemmie, and 'the kittens' and, in the uniform of a major of the Oxford Hussars, crossed the Channel to France. He had resigned from government and intended to join his regiment at the front. On landing he was surprised to find a car waiting to take him to the headquarters of Field Marshal Sir John French, general officer commanding the BEF. When he arrived, he was at once offered either the post of aide-de-camp to French or command of a brigade. His second military career was about to begin.

Churchill declined command of a brigade – a general's appointment – on the grounds of inexperience of conditions on the Western Front. He asked as a preliminary to be posted to a unit in the line where he could learn the ropes. On November 20, 1915, he joined the Second Battalion Grenadier Guards. It was a shrewd move on French's part. The Grenadiers were, and are, the grandest regiment in the British army, of unparalleled fighting reputation and officered by Churchill's social equals. They would stand no nonsense from a former Cabinet minister, and did not. Churchill's kit was ruthlessly simplified – he was left a pair of clean socks and his shaving gear – and he found a battalion headquarters that forbade anything stronger than tea. He thrived nevertheless on the regime, reporting to Clemmie that, despite 'filth and rubbish everywhere, graves built into the defences, water and muck on all sides ... I have found happiness and content such as I have not known for many months.'

During Churchill's first tour in the trenches, of twelve

days, two Grenadiers were killed, two died of wounds, eight were injured. He himself narrowly escaped death when he was unexpectedly called away from a dugout subsequently destroyed by a shell. In early December, French decided that he was now qualified to command a brigade, but was shortly thereafter himself relieved of command. The change had been foreseen by many. French was of moderate ability and highly strung. His laudable insistence on visiting the wounded in hospital progressively depressed him. He wrote touchingly of his tenderness toward the 'brave fellows' he found in the wards, and reproached himself for their sufferings. He should perhaps never have been appointed to high command. His subordinate, General Sir Douglas Haig, had by December 1915 concluded that he should be replaced, and said so to influential people, including the King. French was accordingly removed, to be replaced by Haig himself. Haig at once quashed the proposal that Churchill should be made a brigadier general. Instead he was sent, as a lieutenant colonel, to command a battalion in the trenches, the 6th Royal Scots Fusiliers.

His battalion was 'New Army', a unit of several hundred of the million volunteers of 1914–15. It was utterly unlike the Grenadiers, its soldiers mainly ex-miners, its officers 'young Scots of the middling sort', as he himself described them. He was vastly their social superior, and they found him at first a mystery. He wore odd clothes, including a French steel helmet, supplied himself with hampers from home – demanding from Clemmie 'Stilton, cream, hams, sardines, a big beefsteak pie' – and made grandiloquent speeches. It was only gradually, through displays of his total indifference to danger, that he won his soldiers' respect and eventually affection. They were constantly in and out of the trenches, in a dangerous, waterlogged sector of the front. Churchill insisted on inspecting the trenches, often from no man's land, several times a day. Sometimes he painted. Occasionally he got leave to see Clemmie, and those episodes seem to have been the most passionate of their married life.

Clemmie lobbied incessantly in the political world to secure him a new ministerial appointment. Churchill told her that Asquith was an irreconcilable enemy; Clemmie warned that his real enemy was Lloyd George, 'fair of speech, shifty of eye, treacherous of heart.' Occasionally he visited Parliament, of which he was still a Member. On March 7, 1916, he made a speech in the House. Even Clemmie recognized that his intervention had been a disaster. He had criticized all his old colleagues except Fisher, calling for his return as First Sea Lord. The result was ridicule.

He hoped that he might repair the damage by a second speech and even began to speak of his 'true war station' being at Westminster. Clemmie wisely urged him to return to the battalion, which he did on March 13, remaining with it for the next two months. His heart was not in it, however; after another visit to the House, which had met in secret session, he asked to be released 'to attend to my Parliamentary public duties which have become urgent.' His battalion, in any case, was to be amalgamated with another, which had suffered heavy losses. On May 6, after nearly six months at the front, he left the BEF for good.

Churchill could take justifiable pride in his service with the Royal Scots Fusiliers, which provided a guard at his funeral fifty years after his farewell to them. He had been a devoted commanding officer and often in danger of his life. Yet he had been lucky. Had his political eclipse after the Dardanelles come a little sooner he might have been caught up in the bloody offensive of Loos; had he postponed his departure by six weeks he might have felt honour bound to have joined in the even bloodier offensive on the Somme. His time at the front had, undeliberately, been passed in a military hiatus. As a result, and despite several close brushes with death, he had been spared to remake his political life.

6 War and Peace, 1915–1932

TO REMAKE A political career he had himself done so much to destroy tried all Churchill's talents. His reputation was stained in so many ways: by his change of party, for which the Conservatives had never forgiven him; by his indulgence in controversial journalism; by the showiness of his excursion to Antwerp; above all, by his advocacy of the Dardanelles expedition and its costly failure. The cry 'Dardanelles' followed him wherever he went and spoke, even in the House of Commons. The House can still be a cruel place. The early-twentieth-century House of Commons, centre and hotbed of contemporary politics, could be very cruel indeed. The form of cruelty it chose to show to Churchill after his return from the trenches was studied indifference. He was ignored. When he rose to speak, ministers did not answer. Sometimes they left the chamber, as ordinary Members did also. He had never before failed to command attention. It hurt and humiliated him to find that he could not.

Wounded, he began to exaggerate the traits that had always irritated even his friends. The arrogance and bumptiousness of which his enemies complained became a fact. At this low point in his life, Clemmie came to his aid. She wrote to him, with her characteristic directness, that it was not enough to believe he was in the right, even when he was. He had to take account of others' feelings. He was extravagant in speech and dictatorial in manner and alienated men of ability by his assumption that only he had the right to authority. Moreover, because he thereby put off colleagues who should be his friends, he was left with second-rate companions who encouraged him in bad behaviour. Clemmie called them 'false friends', meaning particularly Max Aitken and F. E. Smith. With his acolyte Brendan Bracken, they were called by her, disparagingly, 'the three Bs'. Clemmie correctly identified all three as careerists, more concerned to use Churchill than to serve him.

Clemmie's wise words may have had some effect, though his depression continued. Her subsequent advice to insist on the right to clear his name of culpability for the Dardanelles bore fruit. Asquith, the prime minister, was brought to agree that the Dardanelles papers should be reviewed by an independent committee. When its findings were published in March 1917, Churchill was cleared of blame for the operation's failure. A great weight was lifted; his resentments dissolved. He began to display again the better side of his character: his resilience, his willingness to forget grievances and to forgive slights and to repair damaged friendships.

By then, moreover, the long-fixed elements in British politics had changed. Asquith, who in his last year as Prime Minister had been characterized by Churchill as 'supine, sodden and supreme', had been driven from office, to be replaced in December 1916 by Lloyd George. The two men, once comrades, then adversaries, became comrades again. In July 1917 Churchill was appointed to Lloyd George's former post as minister of munitions. With work to do, his spirits revived. He threw himself into the management of the war effort, spurring the armaments factories to greater effort, coordinating munitions policy with his French opposite number, and arranging deliveries of guns and shells to the Americans when their troops began to arrive in numbers in France in 1918.

It was humdrum work but important and satisfying, and as he restored his reputation for ministerial competence his prospects improved. In the general election of November 1918, he was returned for Dundee with a large majority. In January 1919, two months after the war ended, he became Secretary of State for War and Air – his interest in flying had never diminished and he had long advocated the creation of a separate Air Ministry – and in January 1921 he became Colonial Secretary. He was to find his hands full.

As war minister he had been much involved in the Allied intervention in Russia, not a policy he had advocated but one he embraced when it became his responsibility. After the collapse of the tsarist government in 1917, Britain had sent thousands of troops to northern Russia, to prevent the large stocks of British war supplies stored there from falling into German hands. When, at the outbreak of the Russian civil war, the Red Bolsheviks chose to regard their White opponents as more dangerous enemies than the Germans, who by complex analysis had in turn come to identify the Bolsheviks as grist for the mill of their military cause, the Western Allies found themselves inextricably involved with the White armies. At the outset neither Churchill nor Lloyd George wanted war with the Bolsheviks. On January 27, 1919, Churchill advised Lloyd George that 'evacuate at once at all costs is a policy ... Reinforce and put the job through is a policy; but unhappily we have not the power.' Between these two well-stated opposites, British policy would oscillate throughout much of 1919, as the fortunes of the Reds and Whites swayed one way and the other. At the outset Churchill seems to have shared Lloyd George's view that it was not for Britain to determine what sort of government Russia should have. When the Reds seemed to be getting the upper hand, he was for negotiating a ceasefire. When the Whites recovered, however, his enthusiasm for supplying them with arms revived also. Lloyd George warned him in September that he had become obsessed by anti-Bolshevism, 'which, if you will forgive me for saying so, is upsetting your balance.' In October, Churchill was still confident that 'the tyranny of Bolshevism will be overthrown by the Russian nation' and authorized the sending of more weapons. A sudden White setback swung him once again toward the idea of compromise. When the final White collapse came at the beginning of 1920, he accepted its implications with reluctance: 'I do not of course believe that any real harmony is possible between Bolshevism and present civilisation. But in view of existing facts we must trust to peaceful influences to bring about the disappearance of this awful tyranny and peril.'

Churchill remained fiercely anti-Communist all his life. His decision of June 1941, immediately after Hitler's invasion of the Soviet Union, to extend the hand of friendship to Joseph Stalin, the Soviet dictator and former Red military commissar, was explicable only in the circumstances. Any enemy of Hitler's he would accept as an ally, he said in his private circle, adding words to the effect that he would sup with the devil if that would aid Britain's cause. He explained his position publicly in more measured terms. 'We shall give whatever help we can to Russia.' The offer, nevertheless, was one of extraordinary personal generosity. A true libertarian, Churchill had a hatred of the Soviet system as genuine as his hatred of Naziism, and of longer date. It took a calculation of extreme expediency for him to set aside his repugnance for all that Stalin represented to recommend him to the British people as a confederate in common adversity. It was a temporary position. In old age, when the war was over, and the guarantee of the American alliance was sure, Churchill would revert, without inconsistency, to the anti-Communism that had been one of the central principles of his political life.

Even while the civil war in Russia was raging, Churchill as Secretary of State for War and Air was deeply involved in another, the civil war in Ireland, where the British army and the local police forces were locked in conflict with Republican nationalists. Ireland had long been the bane of English politics, and Churchill had foreseen that it would become an immediate postwar problem; even as the smoke of the First World War cleared, he perceived 'the dreary steeples of Fermanagh and Tyrone emerging once again.' Those two places stood on the Ulster border, between Protestant and Catholic Ireland. In 1914 the refusal of the Protestant minority to tolerate Home Rule by a Catholic majority had provoked a major political crisis in mainland Britain. The outbreak of the First World War persuaded all those involved in the issue, including the Irish Parliamentary Party, to set their differences aside until the conclusion of the war, in which Irish nationalists played a notably heroic part. Even before it was over, however, Irish Republican intransigents, operating on the principle that 'England's difficulty is Ireland's opportunity,' had raised the standard of revolt. The Easter rising of 1916 was repressed with a severity that outraged even Irish moderates, so that, by 1918, respectable Ireland, outside the Protestant Ulster heartland, was prepared to settle for nothing less than self-government. Westminster foolishly continued to heed Protestant objections and soon found itself with a full-blown insurrection on its hands. Churchill, reared in Lord Randolph's fervent Unionism, argued for fighting things out, and supported the creation of military anti-terror units – the Black and Tans, the 'Auxies' – that adopted the terrorist methods of the Irish Republican Army (IRA). Eventually convinced that the IRA could not be overcome, so strong was its support among the Catholic population, he agreed to accept first the partition of Ireland into a large Catholic South and small Protestant North, then to direct negotiations with the leaders of the IRA to bring about a settlement. In October 1921 he met the IRA emissaries in London. One was Arthur Griffith, a mild idealist, the other Michael Collins, a terrorist with blood on his hands. Churchill's inclination for dealing directly with fighters took charge, as it had twenty years earlier in the making of a peace settlement with the Boer warriors. Churchill and Collins, a member of the Anglo-Irish conference observed, 'appear to fascinate each other and are bosom friends.' Collins complained that he had a price on his head. Churchill produced the Boer poster putting a price on his. In this confederate atmosphere, Collins eventually agreed to a compromise creating an Irish Free State inside the British

Empire. As he put his name to the treaty, he remarked, 'I may have signed my death warrant.' His prescience was acute. The IRA purists would not accept the deed Churchill and Collins had done. Civil war resulted and Collins, the 'Big Fellow', was to die in an anti-Free State ambush in August 1922. 'Tell Winston we could never have done it without him' were almost his last words. His Free State government would survive, with British help. Yet the commander of his killers, Éamon de Valéra, would eventually succeed to power in the new Free State, and transform it in 1948 into the Republic of Ireland, constitutionally committed to the 're-integration' of Ulster into its 'national territory', with doleful consequences that persist to this day. Churchill and de Valéra – who insisted on a pettifogging neutrality during the war against Hitler – were never reconciled. The Big Fellow, by contrast, remained a man close to Churchill's heart, in death as in life, a contradiction of his judgment that 'the Irish have a genius for conspiracy but not for government.'

Ireland was the worst of the problems to confront Churchill in his postwar appointments as Secretary of State for War and then for the Colonies. Its religious communities were irreconcilable and were to remain so, age-old enemies that cherished their mutual hostility. In Palestine, Churchill found a different situation. The territory, long a province of the Ottoman Empire, had passed to British rule by mandate of the League of Nations at the war's end. Though inhabited by an Arab majority, it was historically the homeland of the Jews, who, in 1917, had been made by the British government a promise of return to their 'national home' in Palestine. Churchill, as Colonial Secretary in 1921, found himself the administrator of this so-called Balfour Declaration. He went on a mission to Palestine and came home a convinced Zionist. Speaking to the House of Commons, he assured it that Jewish immigration into the Promised Land would be 'a very slow process and the rights of the existing non-Jewish population would be strictly preserved.' Privately he suspected otherwise; nevertheless he authorized the use of British military force to inaugurate the first wave of Zionist immigration. He was thereby to become an honorary Zionist and to remain so for the rest of his life.

A second, far more violent conflict precipitated by the Ottoman Empire's collapse also greatly occupied Churchill in 1921–22. The Greeks – first of the Ottoman subject peoples to throw off the imperial yoke, at the beginning of the nineteenth century – had long been possessed by the 'Great Idea', the reunification of all the territories where Greeks lived, beyond the borders of the Greek kingdom. The scope of the 'Great Idea' embraced not only the islands fringing the eastern Mediterranean coast of Turkey but parts of the mainland itself, where some cities – Smyrna foremost, and Trabzon on the Black Sea – were largely Greek by population. The collapse of the Turkish army in 1918 prompted the Greek government to embark on a campaign of conquest. At the outset it was successful. Then Kemal, the general who had defeated the British landings at the Dardanelles in 1915, collected forces and launched a counteroffensive. Although outnumbered, the Turks routed the Greeks and drove them back to the sea. Turkey's Greek population fled; Smyrna, a city of a million people, was burned out. The Turkish advance eventually brought Kemal's troops into contact with the British Army of the Black Sea, which was garrisoning Constantinople and the Dardanelles, pending the signing of a peace treaty.

Lloyd George, as Prime Minister, determined to prevent Kemal's troops from crossing the Dardanelles. Churchill supported him, but Britain's allies did not: France and Italy withdrew their troops. Australia and Canada, furious at not being consulted before the decision to make a stand was taken, refused a British request to send help. For some weeks in September 1922 the prospect of a new war between Britain and Turkey loomed. Churchill, previously pro-Turk, and anxious to settle the hostilities which had opened in October 1914 by a 'generous peace', became possessed anew by his old Dardanelles fever. He was horrified by the Turkish barbarities at Smyrna – partly provoked by the retreating Greek army's commission of widespread atrocities against Turkish villagers – and alarmed by the prospect of Turkey's re-establishing its power on the European mainland. Nevertheless he backed Lloyd George throughout the crisis, which was resolved when Kemal chose not to come to blows with the British. A peace treaty, signed at Lausanne in July 1923, restored Constantinople, renamed Istanbul, to the Turks. Kemal, henceforth also Atatürk, 'Father of the Turks', became president of the reconstituted Turkish state. It exchanged its isolated populations for those of Greece, greatly to the disadvantage of the Greeks, since theirs much outnumbered Turkey's. The settlement nevertheless restored order to the eastern Mediterranean world. It put an end to the fantasy of the 'Great Idea', created the conditions in which Atatürk brought Turkey into modern international society, and established the diplomatic relations that would neutralize Hitler's efforts to make it a German ally again during the Second World War. Churchill's over-emotional relationship with the Dardanelles was to bear fruit in the end, through

Turkey's meticulously maintained neutrality in the struggle between the contestants for control of the straits in 1939–45.

By 1923 Churchill was out of office, indeed out of Parliament. Since the general election of 1918 Lloyd George had led a coalition in which Conservatives greatly outnumbered members of his own Liberal Party, to which Churchill still belonged. In October 1922 the Conservatives rebelled against Liberal leadership and ousted Lloyd George as Prime Minister. In the subsequent general election, Churchill lost his Dundee seat, and he lost again in November 1923, when Stanley Baldwin, the new Conservative Prime Minister, called a second election. Baldwin had been defeated in the Commons by a combination of the surviving Liberals and the Labour Party, now a real political force. Labour was not yet attractive enough to the electorate to secure a national mandate, but it emerged from the election with enough seats to form, with Liberal support, a government. Churchill was alarmed by Labour's rise. Despite his commitment in youth to Liberal welfarism, he feared Labour's tenderness toward the Soviet Union and its increasingly socialist economic policy. He also doubted the capacity of the Liberal Party to restore itself as an effective party of opposition. During 1924 he began to adjust his political position, first offering to bring the support of the anti-Labour Liberals to the Conservatives in parliament, then speaking directly to Conservative constituency associations, as if he were offering himself as a candidate. In April he told the Liverpool Conservatives that their party alone could defeat socialism. In September, though still technically a Liberal, he accepted nomination for the safe Conservative seat of Epping, a

London suburb. In October the Labour Prime Minister, Ramsay MacDonald, was forced to call yet another general election. In his manifesto to the Epping voters, Churchill declared, 'I give my whole support to the Conservative Party.' He was returned with a majority of nine thousand and was to hold the seat (later renamed Woodford) for the rest of his parliamentary life.

Churchill was later to make a joke of his erratic party allegiance; he had now crossed the floor twice. He returned to the Conservative Party with no expectation of prompt preferment to office. 'I think it very likely that I shall not be invited to join the government,' he wrote at the time, 'as owing to the size of the majority it will probably be composed only of impeccable Conservatives.' Impeccable he certainly was not; sincere he may yet be thought. Despite the then strong, and long-lingering, suspicion that he had left the Conservatives because the electoral mood doomed them to years out of office and had rejoined them again because by then it was the Liberals who looked the spent force, there was consistency in his conduct. Churchill, unlike most public men of the contemporary upper class, had strong political beliefs. Though not an intellectual, he was philosophically a libertarian who also held that the state had a responsibility to provide for the welfare of its poorer citizens. It was the welfare issue, characterized by him as 'Tory democracy', that had impelled him to change sides in 1904. In 1924 it was his libertarianism. He took the Labour Party's rhetoric at face value, recoiled from its commitment to expropriation and nationalization, and suspected its internationalist foreign policy. The Liberals having lost their electoral following, he recognized that only the Conservatives could effectively oppose Labour in Parliament. It was for that reason that he crossed the floor a second time.

He was wrong to suppose that he would be barred from office. Though Churchill was indeed distrusted by the 'impeccable Conservatives', Stanley Baldwin, again Prime Minister, was a wholly undogmatic leader who recognized Churchill's worth. Immediately after his return to power, he summoned Churchill to see him. Clemmie urged Winston to accept the Ministry of Health, if offered. To his astonishment Baldwin asked him to become Chancellor of the Exchequer, one of the great offices of state. The invitation seemed to confirm his return to the political mainstream.

So it might have done, in different circumstances. Churchill, though personally spendthrift and apparently incapable of managing his own money on any but a hand-to-mouth basis, had a good understanding of the orthodoxies of public finance. A lifelong free-trader, he knew that fixed exchange rates, linked to the price of gold, allowed goods to circulate in a competitive market that kept prices down. Interference with the exchange rate, particularly by taxing imports or subsidizing exports, although superficially an alternative means of protecting the interests of home producers, ultimately damaged the general prosperity by driving foreign governments to tax and subsidize in return. The resulting managed markets were inferior to the free market, which, in theory, benefited all who traded in it. So orthodoxy said; in the conditions prevailing, however, after the First World War, which had laden the economies of victors and vanquished alike with huge internal but also international war debts, the free market was distorted by interest payments. Much of the taxation raised in Britain, for example, went to service the American war loan of five billion dollars, perhaps five hundred billion today. The burden would have been manageable, and the capital repayable, had Britain's own war debtors – notably France – been willing to repay. They demurred, thus tempting postwar British governments to recoup by taxing imports. The temporary relief ensuing was cancelled when the debtor nations taxed exports from Britain in return.

Churchill, as Chancellor, was advised by his Treasury officials and the Bank of England to break the deadlock by 'returning to the Gold Standard', which would henceforth automatically set the price at which goods were sold on the international market. The move was sound in theory; in practice, because it was not reciprocated by Britain's debtors, export prices rose, putting manufacturers into difficulty and leading them to seek a reduction in wages. Churchill was not sympathetic. In his first budget he had returned to his policy of 'Tory democracy', introducing measures to increase pension and unemployment payments and to liberalize the conditions under which they were made. Caught thereafter between the demands of employers and the intransigence of the unions, particularly the Miners' Union, he could offer no way out. In May 1926 the Trades Union Congress called a general strike in support of their miner comrades. During the nine days the strike lasted, he strenuously opposed it, taking charge of the *British Gazette*, put out by the government while the newspaper unions struck. In the aftermath his advice was wholly conciliatory. He condemned the mine owners for their harshness and supported the introduction of a minimum wage, 'below which on social grounds miners ought not to work'; many of Churchill's soldiers in the 6th

Royal Scots Fusiliers had been miners. His patrician concern for the welfare of the working class is now forgotten, as it was during much of his later life. Genuine it was nevertheless. In ampler economic times he would have won a durable reputation as a populist Chancellor.

The economic climate dictated that he did not, even though he introduced five budgets, none hostile to the interests of the working class. Patriot though he was – patriotism, even more than liberty in political and economic life, was his central political principle – he opposed increases in the naval budget and sought generally for reductions in public expenditure, except in the direction of public welfare. He remained, as he had begun, a champion of the working man, but now in the wrong party. He was quite at odds with the social policy of the Conservatives. Their defeat in the general election of 1929 may have spared him another conflict with party leadership. In 1929 Labour was elected a second time. Ramsay MacDonald proved incapable of dealing with the economic crises that, on a worldwide scale, engulfed Britain's government shortly thereafter. Nevertheless, when forced to call a general election in 1931, MacDonald remained Prime Minister, as head of a National Government composed of his few Labour and Liberal supporters and more than four hundred Conservatives. Churchill was one of them but was not offered office, nor was he to hold any post for the rest of the peacetime 1930s. At first it was his opposition to the government's plans for further devolution of power within the Indian empire that disfavoured him. Thereafter, and progressively, it was his strident warnings of the danger presented by the rise of Naziism in Germany and his vociferous demands for rearmament that isolated him in Parliament. The more strongly he felt and spoke, the lonelier he was to become.

As the 'wilderness years' extended, he found consolation in his private interests, particularly writing, which proved increasingly profitable. He had completed *The World Crisis*, his history of the First World War, in 1929. In 1930 he also published *My Early Life*, a lighthearted and still delightfully readable memoir of his youth at school, Sandhurst, and in the army, which reveals much of his character and aspirations. In the previous year he had begun his life of Marlborough, eventually to extend to four volumes, which remains the most substantial of his literary works. It was not written without difficulty, however. In 1929 he had lost heavily in the American stock market crash, but he had returned to the United States in 1931 to recoup on a highly paid lecture tour. In New York, on December 13 of that year, he was knocked down by a car on Fifth Avenue, tossed into the gutter, and severely injured. The fault, he freely admitted, was his own; he had looked the wrong way as he stepped off to cross the street. The accident left him cut to the bone on his scalp and badly bruised. He went with Clemmie to the Bahamas to convalesce. From Nassau she wrote to their son, Randolph, that he was 'very sad', and said that he had now in the last two years had three heavy blows. 'First the loss of all that money in the crash, then the loss of his political position in the Conservative Party, and now this terrible physical injury. He said he did not think he would ever recover completely from the three events.'

His misfortunes continued. While recovering from the car accident, he came down with paratyphoid fever and, after appearing better, suffered a relapse. The illness was a perpetuation of an alarming Churchillian trait: susceptibility to illness or life-threatening accident. He had been a sickly child; had nearly died of pneumonia (an illness that was to recur) at the age of fourteen in 1888; had suffered a serious fall when he threw himself off the bridge at Deepdene to avoid capture in a boyish game; had nearly drowned in Lake Geneva while swimming off a boat; and had had a series of falls from horses and polo accidents, culminating in the dislocation of a shoulder, already damaged on army service, which then became chronic. He had had appendicitis during an Oldham by-election and had twice survived failures of primitive aircraft during his unsuccessful effort to win his pilot's license. Surprisingly, he had not been wounded in action, though he courted danger whenever it offered. He was also prone to bouts of depression – 'black dog', as he called it; though their frequency diminished as his life protracted, he could never be certain that they would not recur.

He possessed, nevertheless, extraordinary resilience. Soon after the New York accident and the paratyphoid episode, he got back to work on *Marlborough*. He also conceived the idea of writing a history of the English-speaking peoples, uniting that of his father's nation with his mother's country, and soon arranged a highly profitable contract, a quarter (five thousand pounds) payable in advance. Money always cheered Churchill up. The book would not see the light of day for nearly twenty years. In the interval it helped to sustain his perennially extravagant way of life. Large houses (he was now living in and expensively improving Chartwell, the manor in Kent he had bought in 1922), cruises, foreign holidays, opulent motor cars (though he had been given a

Daimler by friends after his accident), dinners, grand hotels, squads of secretaries and servants, the best schools for his children, silk underwear and Havana cigars for himself, champagne for his guests – all the ingredients of ducal life – seem to have been necessary to Churchill's well-being. Although politically in the wilderness after 1931, when Ramsay MacDonald formed his National Government without a place for Churchill, he continued to live very well, if on tenterhooks about finding the means to carry off appearances. Articles were written for his press-baron friends, delivered by the chauffeur with orders to wait for the cheque. Creditors were stared down. Somehow he swam rather than sank.

He had lost over India, which was granted a major measure of domestic self-government despite the success of his appeal to Conservative imperial instincts in 1931. From 1932 onward he found a new cause: resistance to the rise of totalitarian politics in Germany. During his research for his Marlborough biography, visiting the duke's Bavarian battlefields, he had almost had a meeting with Hitler in Munich. Despite the near-miss, he had detected the feel of Naziism nonetheless. In February 1933, a month after Hitler became chancellor, Churchill, speaking in Oxford, evoked Germany's new spirit. 'I think of Germany with its splendid clear-eyed youth marching forward on all the roads of the Reich, singing their ancient songs, demanding to be conscripted into an army; eagerly seeking the most terrible weapons of war; burning to suffer and die for their fatherland.' The menace of renascent German militarism was to be Churchill's theme for the next six years of his political and parliamentary life.

7 The Coming of War, 1933–1940

CHURCHILL'S POLITICAL LIFE thus far had been associated with particular causes: Tory democracy first, then social reform, last of all 'the Dardanelles', a cry that was to haunt him throughout his later forties and fifties. After 1932, when he became fifty-eight, an age at which most politicians enter into decline, he espoused a new cause, opposition to appeasement, that was to carry him to political greatness.

Appeasement as a policy was slow to take form, developing only in response to the attack on democracy mounted by the totalitarian regimes. Totalitarian politics, the dominant movement of the 1930s, was a politics of grievance. First manifest in Italy, where Benito Mussolini capitalized on popular dissatisfaction with Italy's share of the spoils of victory to overthrow liberal government in 1922, it next took root in Japan, which felt itself disfavoured by Anglo-American measures of postwar naval disarmament, and then in Germany, when Adolf Hitler, leader of the ultranationalist Nazi party, secured a parliamentary majority in January 1933. The totalitarian idea made no room for opposition in the electoral system; though sometimes calling itself socialist, as the Nazi party did in Germany, it was violently opposed to the Bolshevik socialism of the Russian Communists. It was also fiercely and radically imperialist; Mussolini's fascist state embarked on the creation of an Italian African empire in 1936, and Japan's military regime revealed its inner nature by its assault on China in 1937. Nazi Germany – restrained at first by the measures of disarmament imposed by the Versailles treaty – was slower to show its hand. In 1935, however, it unilaterally revoked the clause of the Versailles treaty forbidding conscription and limiting its army to a strength of one hundred thousand; in 1936 its burgeoning army reoccupied the demilitarized Rhineland; by 1937, with a growing air force and a new U-boat fleet, it possessed sufficient military strength to challenge France and Britain on equal terms. Neither wanted nor was ready for war. Both responded to Hitler by seeking to placate rather than confront him, and more ignobly as his demands grew more extortionate. 'Appeasement' took definite shape only in 1936, but its outlines were detectable much earlier, and were recognized and denounced by Churchill in the first days of the Nazi seizure of power. It was that prescience that earned him, if in retrospect, his title as the twentieth century's great champion of liberty.

What Churchill saw, others did not. The great issues in British politics in the first half of the 1930s were imperial and economic, not strategic. Both were distractions from the growing military crisis. The Government of India Bill, drafted to devolve power within the Indian empire to elected assemblies in its provinces, engaged much of the passion and prejudice of the Conservative members of the National Government between 1932 and 1935. Churchill resolutely opposed the bill's passage, thus heightening his isolation inside the party. He was less embroiled in economic concerns, though taxation and expenditure were the chief determinants of the government's strategic policy during the early Hitler years. Churchill saw only military needs. His opponents – particularly Neville Chamberlain, Chancellor of the Exchequer from 1931 to 1937 – were oppressed by the burdens of unemployment, industrial decline, falling exports, and an adverse balance of payments. Hindsight reproaches them with unconcern for national security. Contemporary realities explain their desire to spend what money could be raised by revenue on import penalty, export subsidy, unemployment relief, and balancing the budget.

The critical event in British politics in the early 1930s was not, as later judgment suggests, Hitler's seizure of power in Germany in 1933 but the collapse of the national economy in 1931. It was an effect of the world economic crisis that began with the American stock market crash of 1929 but that then progressively destroyed the prosperity of all countries belonging to the international trading system, together with that of their colonial possessions. Even the Soviet Union, though apparently sheltered from market forces by the separation of its economy from capitalist mechanisms, suffered. In Britain, the third largest economy in the world after those of the United States and Germany, the effects of the slump were devastating. Unemployment reached nearly three million in January 1933, out of a potential workforce of twenty million. Of the unemployed, nearly a million were 'chronic', those beyond their most vigorous years or else seeking work in the traditional industries – mining, iron and steel production, shipbuilding, textiles – for which bulk markets no longer existed.

Worse than the slump itself was its effect on popular perceptions of Britain's state and on official efforts to bring back better times, effectively the Victorian golden age, falsely remembered. The British felt badly off during the 1930s. They were oppressed by the spectacle of honest working men, many veterans of the First World War, tramping to London in 'hunger marches' from what the government had defined as Depressed Areas, where traditional industry had collapsed. Those in public employment – teachers, civil servants, military men – were alarmed by statutory reductions of their pay. The spectre of poverty hung over the country, and its threat was enhanced by governmental measures enacted to hold it at bay, notably the 10 per cent reduction in public salaries enforced in 1931 and the imposition of tariffs on nonimperial imports imposed in March 1932.

Public alarm was unfounded. The 1930s were eventually to prove, public perception to the contrary, a prosperous decade. Outside the Depressed Areas – the Welsh mining valleys, the Scottish Lowlands, the shipbuilding centres in Cumberland and Tyneside – most of Britain enjoyed a modest boom. There was a considerable migration of the young unemployed to regions of new industry in the Midlands and the London area, stimulating housebuilding and the output of products new homeowners desired, particularly electrical goods and motor cars. Unemployment fell during the 1930s; real wages rose. The British felt badly off only because they empathized with the misfortunes of those objectively badly off, a shrinking minority.

Nevertheless the after-effects of the world crash and the subsequent British slump set the tone for British politics in what, for Churchill, would be his Wilderness Years. Neville Chamberlain, Chancellor of the Exchequer for most of the period, took it as his responsibility to protect by every means the slow process of industrial recovery. That required, as he saw it, the least onerous tax regime possible and the most parsimonious programme of public spending. Defence had, historically, been the heaviest drain on the public purse. Under his chancellorship the services were starved of funds. He denied the Royal Navy new capital ships and the Royal Air Force modern aircraft. The army was left in an almost archaic state, with equipment suitable only for conducting colonial operations. What new money the air force got went to buy bombers, though that was not Chamberlain's fault. Its senior officers had mistakenly committed themselves to the view that Britain's best defence against air attack lay in the acquisition of offensive means, a policy so belatedly reversed that it was only by the narrowest of margins that Fighter Command acquired the Spitfires and Hurricanes which would win the Battle of Britain in 1940.

Meanwhile, under Hitler, Germany was transforming itself into the world's leading military power. The Versailles treaty of 1919 had deprived it of an air force, had denied its navy capital ships and submarines, and had left it with only a token army, forbidden to possess heavy artillery and tanks. Step by step, after his elevation to the chancellorship in January 1933, Hitler set about reversing Germany's military humiliation. In October 1934 he ordered the German army to begin building a tank fleet. In March 1935 he decreed the creation of an air force, the Luftwaffe, the elements of which were already in existence. In 1936 he persuaded the British government to accept an alteration of the Versailles treaty that would allow Germany to build and deploy submarines. The most menacing of Hitler's rearmament measures, however, was his decision in March 1935 to reintroduce conscription. At a stroke, a German army artificially restricted to inferior status vis-à-vis its neighbours began to expand, first to match and then to exceed their strengths. In 1934 the Reichsheer was outnumbered by the Polish and Czech armies, greatly outnumbered by the French, even outnumbered by the British, and completely outmatched by the Red Army. Within the next three years, however, the balance of military power in Europe would be transformed. By September 1938 the German army, which in 1933 possessed only seven infantry and three cavalry divisions, stood at a strength of forty-six infantry divisions and five panzer (tank) divisions, with a numerical strength of six hundred thousand. By comparison the British army had only six infantry divisions and one notional tank division; many of its two hundred thousand soldiers were dispersed abroad in colonial garrisons. The Luftwaffe, with three thousand combat aircraft, already outnumbered both the Royal Air Force and the Armée de l'Air. The French army, though large, was hidebound and poorly equipped.

'Thank God for the French army,' Churchill was to remark as his fears of German rearmament grew. By December 1938 he had become aware that in 1940 'the annual contingent [of recruits] in Germany would be double that of France.' It was the realization of his fears, which he had begun to voice even before Hitler achieved power. They were first aroused by the German response to the World Disarmament Conference of 1932. Germany, then still under democratic government, demanded parity of armaments with France. Churchill told the Commons in July, 'I should very much regret to see any approximation of military strength between Germany and France.' In March 1933, with Hitler installed as head of government in Germany, Churchill began to express anxiety about Britain's unconcern for its own security. As an economy measure, proposed to foster industrial recovery, the British government announced a plan to reduce spending on the air force for the second year running. 'Not to have an adequate air force in the present state of the world,' he warned, 'is to compromise the foundations of national freedom and independence.'

In March 1932 one of his objects had been achieved. The government had agreed to drop the Ten-Year Rule, imposed in 1919, that no major war was to be expected in that period. It had been extended year by year, since 1928. Its abandonment, however, brought no major measure of British rearmament. In October 1933 he supported a motion proposed at the conference of the Conservative Party, expressing 'grave anxiety' at the depressed state of the country's defences. Though it carried unanimously, the National Government, effectively controlled by the Conservatives, responded to Germany's withdrawal from the World Disarmament Conference on October 14 by reaffirming its commitment to the search for a reduction of world armaments and, shortly afterwards, by encouraging the French government to placate Germany by mutual arms limitation.

Churchill began to demand the doubling of the air force, and then its doubling again. He was unaware that the chief of the Air Staff, in July 1934, had unsuccessfully demanded of the Cabinet exactly the same thing. Many ordinary British people supported him. None in government would, however; even Anthony Eden, a rising Conservative star and his future stalwart, differed. Churchill, he told the Commons, 'seems to conceive that in order to have an effective world consultative system nations have to be heavily armed. I do not agree.' Clement Attlee, the Labour leader, who was to become Churchill's wartime deputy, told the Commons in the same debate, 'I think we can generally say today that [Hitler's] dictatorship is gradually breaking down.'

Such self-delusion was almost universal among Britain's political class in the early Hitler years. Its members, many of whom had fought in the First World War, shrank from any thought of a repetition, to which rearmament appeared a preliminary, besides also being destructive of the country's fragile economic reawakening. While many privately shared Churchill's anxieties, they were unwilling publicly to break ranks. Fortunately for the security of the country, there were some among their subordinates who were prepared to act otherwise. Loyalty to the code of ministerial authority is one of the foundation stones of the British governmental system. Career civil servants, regular officers – the agents of efficient continuity in British administrative life – obediently subordinate their better instincts to official policy, however ill judged it may appear. However, as the 1930s drew on, and the looming awfulness of a Europe dominated by Hitler became ever clearer in outline, Britain's official class demurred. In a wholly uncharacteristic exercise of bureaucratic impropriety, one senior official after another began secretly to supply Churchill – with potentially disastrous consequences for their own careers – with secret information that lent unarguable substance to his warnings.

They included Major Desmond Morton, head of the industrial intelligence section of the Committee of Imperial Defence, the forerunner of the Ministry of Defence; Orme Sargent and Ralph Wigram, of the Foreign Office; Squadron Leaders Charles Anderson and Herbert Rowles, of the RAF; and Brigadier Percy Hobart, commander of the Tank Corps. Most brought details of the backwardness of Britain's air defence program, but Reginald Leeper, head of the Foreign Office Information Department, also wrote with an urgent request for Churchill to speak on behalf of the recently formed Anti-Nazi Council, to respond to German propaganda and uphold the values of democracy. His was a startling breach of protocol – civil servants being bound not to oppose public policy – and evidence of how widely Churchill's anxieties were shared by those privy to the government's secrets.

The cabinet, it must be recognized in fairness, did during 1934 take steps to reverse some of the damage done by more than a decade of underspending on defence. It accepted a report that placed the needs of the air force at the head of a list of requirements and, to the dismay of the proponents of bombing in the Air Ministry, gave priority to the procurement of new fighters and other air defence measures. It was still preoccupied, however, with the need to nurture industrial revival and refused to make large increases in the defence budget. As late as December 1937, Sir Thomas Inskip, recently appointed minister for the coordination of defence, a post of considerably lesser importance than that of minister of defence, the creation of which Churchill had long advocated, was still telling the cabinet that increased defence spending threatened to upset credit and the balance of payments.

The government then in office was formally Conservative, that party having won a large majority in the general election of 1935. Baldwin, Prime Minister for the third time, had made no place for Churchill in his ministerial appointments, nor was there a demand from the back benches to find him one. Churchill always filled the chamber when he spoke, and his speeches were privately admired, but his message was too uncomfortable and too much at variance with official policy to command parliamentary support. Moreover an aura of unreliability still clung to him. Conventional Conservatives too easily regarded Churchill as 'unsound'. That reputation had unfortunately been enhanced at the end of 1936, when he had taken King Edward VIII's side over his desire to marry the twice-divorced American, Mrs Wallis Simpson. In the abdication crisis that resulted, Churchill sought ways to make it constitutionally possible for the King both to marry and to remain on the throne. In so doing he made a double misjudgement. The mood of the country, which Churchill failed to perceive, was strongly against the marriage, while the King, as later became apparent, wished to remain on the throne only insofar as Mrs Simpson wished to be his official consort. It is now known that she did not, and that he set her whims quite above his duties.

Churchill's maladroitness during the abdication crisis set back his claim to speak in the common interest precisely at the moment when military and international affairs in

Europe began to take a still more dangerous turn. Before 1937 Hitler's aggressiveness had been directed inward, against individuals and groups inside the country whom he identified as enemies of himself, his party, or the new Germany. From 1937 on, his aggressions turned outward, against countries that contained German minorities, possessed sizeable Nazi parties, or included territory that had been German before 1918. They were, specifically, Czechoslovakia, Austria, and Poland. Hitler also had longer-term geopolitical ambitions, including that of making major conquests in the East for German *Lebensraum* (living space), as he had outlined in his political manifesto, *Mein Kampf.* In the mean time, however, his aims were more immediate and lay close to home.

No part of Czechoslovakia had ever been German territory. The country had been formed in 1919 from three Austro-Hungarian possessions, Bohemia, Moravia, and part of Galicia. Most of its citizens were Slavs. Its western borderland, however, the Sudetenland, was solidly German and the Sudetenlanders chafed under Slav rule. The local Nazi party demanded secession to Germany and was strongly supported. Hitler, who detested the 'succession states' of the Versailles treaty, saw in Sudetenlander dissidence a chance to humiliate the Czechs, to add to the size and strength of what he was already calling 'Greater Germany', and to weaken the victors of 1918. Czechoslovakia was a French ally, part of the Little Entente of Eastern European states set up after Versailles as a counterweight to any revival of German military power. It had a strong army, advanced military industries, and a dense line of fortifications, situated in the Sudetenland frontier with Germany. If the Sudetenland could be detached from Czechoslovakia, Hitler would simultaneously undermine both the Little Entente and French domestic security.

That Czechoslovakia was a potential victim of Hitler's diplomatic aggression became obvious in the spring of 1938. It was not, however, the first of the successor states to fall. In February the Austrian prime minister, Kurt Schuschnigg, in response to Nazi pressure for an Anschluss, the integration of his country with Germany, announced a national plebiscite on the issue. Before it could be held, Hitler, on March 11, marched his troops across the frontier. In Vienna exultant crowds cheered their entry. Leading anti-Nazi Austrians fled, went into hiding, or were arrested. In the aftermath of the invasion, Austria ceased to exist as an independent state. Its army was integrated into Germany's, and its administration consigned to a Nazi appointee.

The Anschluss greatly weakened Czechoslovakia's military situation. Its richest part, the old Kingdom of Bohemia, was now surrounded by 'Greater Germany' on three sides. France declared its intention to assist the Czechs if they suffered unprovoked aggression. Churchill, speaking in the Commons, urged Britain to join in 'a solemn treaty for mutual defence against aggression' under the League of Nations covenant. 'If it were done,' he urged, 'in the year 1938 – and believe me it may be the last chance there will be for doing it – then I say that you might even now arrest this approaching war … [L]et those who wish to reject it ponder well and earnestly upon what will happen to us, if when all else has been thrown to the wolves, we are left to face our fate alone.'

This theme, of facing fate alone, anticipated Churchill's great summertime speeches of 1940; it may be that he had a premonition of what fate held in store. In the spring of 1938, however, he still hoped that accelerated rearmament and making common cause with France and perhaps Russia might deter Hitler from further action. In his private life, despite his anxieties, he remained as creative as ever, working on the last volume of *Marlborough* and the first of *The English-Speaking Peoples*. He also wrote widely for the newspapers, about the gathering menace in Central Europe. In September the spectre of his fears took tangible form. It became clear that Hitler was determined to seize the Sudetenland by one means or another. On September 15 Chamberlain, who had succeeded Baldwin as Prime Minister on May 28, flew to Berchtesgaden, Hitler's mountain retreat, to discuss the terms to be offered to the Czech government. It was the first of several meetings he was to hold with the dictator. At the third, in Munich on September 29, he, the French premier, Édouard Daladier, and Mussolini confirmed the details. Those parts of the Sudetenland with a German majority were to be transferred at once; plebiscites in the other parts would determine their future. The Czech government, excluded from the talks, was presented with a fait accompli.

On October 5 Churchill spoke on the Munich agreement in the Commons. It remains one of the greatest of his speeches. 'All is over,' he began. 'Silent, mournful, abandoned, broken, Czechoslovakia recedes into the darkness.' He went on to review the consequences of surrender to Hitler:

I have tried my best to urge the maintenance of every bulwark of defence – first the timely creation of a [superior] Air Force; secondly the gathering together of the collective strength of many nations; and thirdly, the making of alliances ... all within the [League of Nations] Covenant ... It has all been in vain. Every position has been successively undermined, and abandoned on specious and plausible excuse.

He declared, 'I do not grudge our loyal, brave people ... the spontaneous outburst of joy and relief when they learned that the hard ordeal would no longer be required of them at the moment.' The announcement of the Munich agreement had been greeted with widespread enthusiasm, at the end of a month when air-raid trenches had been dug in public parks and a trial evacuation of the nation's city children to the safety of the countryside had been staged. 'But,' he went on, 'they should know the truth. They should know that there has been gross neglect and deficiency in our defences; they should know that we have sustained a defeat without war ... they should know that we have passed an awful milestone in our history, when the whole equilibrium of Europe has been deranged ... And,' he concluded, 'do not suppose that this is the end. This is only the first sip, the first foretaste of a bitter cup which will be proffered to us year by year unless by a supreme recovery of moral health and martial vigour, we arise again and take our stand for freedom as in the olden time.'

Churchill's consistency of purpose and magnificent oratory were now beginning to weaken the control exerted by the Conservative leadership over its Commons majority. At the vote on the Munich debate, thirty Conservative members abstained. They included several former ministers – Anthony Eden, Duff Cooper – who had resigned from the government to join Churchill in protest against the official policy of appeasement. They remained, nevertheless, a minority. Chamberlain continued to resist bringing confrontation with Germany to a head, and many in the party and the country supported his refusal. Moreover, Chamberlain had a degree of reason on his side; however reluctantly, he had at last been brought to accept that rearmament was a pressing necessity, whatever the budgetary damage done to the national economy. By 1938 Fighter Command was procuring hundreds of the new, fast, heavily armed Hurricane and Spitfire monoplanes, the equal of anything the Luftwaffe deployed, while the Air Defence of Great Britain, a branch of the Air Ministry, was rapidly completing its Home Chain network of early-warning radar stations, together with the control centres necessary to coordinate warning signals with fighter responses. In a sense Churchill was, during 1938, getting ahead of himself. He was demanding a confrontation with Germany that was better postponed until Britain's defences were stronger than the pace of rearmament permitted.

Hitler, however, was also forcing the pace. On March 15, 1939, his troops marched eastward from the Sudetenland to occupy Czechoslovakia proper. That night he slept in Prague. The Czech half of Czechoslovakia was deemed to be a German protectorate, while Slovakia became a German puppet state. On March 25 Chamberlain, affronted by Hitler's abrogation of the Munich Agreement and recognizing that Churchill's warnings of the 'bitter cup' had substance, unilaterally extended a diplomatic guarantee to Poland – then inarguably the next target of Nazi aggression – which committed Britain to military action if the Poles were attacked. France joined in. Soviet Russia, invited to do likewise, made conditions the

Poles would not accept. Germany was now pressing the Poles to agree to the reintegration of Danzig, a Versailles 'free city' inside Polish territory, into Germany. The Poles demurred. Hitler began to make military dispositions. During May, June, and July the British and French conferred, dilatorily, with the Russians over plans for mutual assistance. They made little progress. Then, in August, Stalin, through his foreign minister, Vyacheslav Molotov, made a direct approach to Hitler. The Soviet Union, like Germany, harbored grievances against the Poles. The Versailles treaty had given Poland territory the Russians thought theirs, and they had fought and won a war to hold on to it. On August 22 Molotov and Joachim von Ribbentrop, Hitler's foreign minister, signed a non-aggression pact. It contained a secret clause partitioning Poland between the two nations in case of war. Hitler, now relieved of the danger of fighting on two fronts, resolved on action. Without further negotiation with Warsaw, he launched an invasion on September 1. The Polish army, facing the Germans on three sides, began to collapse almost at once.

Chamberlain nevertheless hesitated to invoke the guarantee to Poland; so did France. He proposed convening a conference if Germany would agree to withdraw its troops. At that the House of Commons lost patience. The Labour members effectively demanded a declaration of war. Even Chamberlain's Cabinet colleagues, appeasers almost to a man, took the same line in private. On September 2 Chamberlain agreed to issue an ultimatum next morning. When it ran out without a response from Berlin, Britain found itself at war with Germany for the second time in the century. A French ultimatum also ran out unanswered that afternoon.

Churchill, who had been offered a place in the War Cabinet on September 1, refrained from speaking or acting during this fraught period, explaining to friends that he felt himself to be a member of the government. But Chamberlain then did not make good his offer. It was not until after the expiration of the ultimatum that he appointed Churchill First Lord of the Admiralty. Churchill found little to do. While Germany completed the destruction of Poland, also invaded by Russia on September 17, the British and French armies proceeded methodically with mobilization; neither country took air or naval action against Germany, however. During the autumn a 'phoney war' set in. The French army manned the Maginot Line facing the enemy; a small British Expeditionary Force went to France. Throughout a harsh winter and cold spring the Allied troops confined themselves to bombarding the Siegfried Line and mounting raids into no man's land. Meanwhile the Russians occupied the Baltic states and attacked Finland, whose gallant resistance the Allies seriously considered supporting. Before they could do so, Finland surrendered. Hitler shortly initiated his own Baltic and North Sea operation, invading Denmark and Norway on April 9, 1940. Tiny Denmark was overrun immediately. The geography of Norway allowed its gallant army to put up a longer resistance, with French and British assistance. Their operations aroused Churchill's enthusiasm, and the Royal Navy won a striking victory at the Second Battle of Narvik, which halved the size of the German surface fleet. The land campaign was, however, lacklustre. As it dragged on, with the Germans gradually gaining the upper hand, both the country and the Commons began to articulate a dissatisfaction with the current leadership that Chamberlain could no longer ignore. On May 7, 1940, a debate on Norway opened in the House. There were two days of stormy argument, ending in an effective vote of no confidence. Chamberlain, humiliated, left the chamber to shouted demands for his resignation. He tried on May 9 to win support for a new, all-party government, but Labour made it clear they would not serve under him. His suggestion that Lord Halifax might replace him, put to Churchill, met a studied silence. On May 10 Chamberlain tendered his resignation to King George VI. Asked to name his successor, he advised that it must be Churchill. His advice was constitutionally binding, and that evening Winston went to Buckingham Palace and returned as Prime Minister.

8   A Prime Minister Alone, 1940–1941

IT IS NOW often thought that Churchill became Prime Minister because of the success of the German blitzkrieg, which produced the strategic catastrophe against which he had warned throughout the appeasement years. It is ironic, in retrospect, to perceive that the appeasers were brought down by their mishandling of the comparatively insignificant sideshow in Norway, leaving Churchill to inherit the catastrophe he had argued so long to avert, during the first hours of its unrolling. Churchill became a wartime prime minister – at the age of sixty-five – in the fire of crisis, without a moment given to him to consider policy or even to learn the routine of office.

Every prime minister, however, to some extent makes his own routine, and so it was with Churchill. Unfortunately for those closest to him, the timetable he chose was very much that he had fixed while living the life of a writer at Chartwell in the 1930s. It began early and extended into the small hours. Waking at eight, after only six hours' sleep, he ate a large breakfast – partridge, pheasant, or steak – in bed, read the newspapers, and considered official papers. (These included raw intelligence intercepts from Bletchley Park, the decryption centre in Buckinghamshire, material called by him 'Boniface'.) Then he began to dictate to his secretaries, one of them taking down his words direct onto a 'silent Remington' typewriter. From time to time he would demand to see the text, correcting peremptorily.

Rising in the late morning, he dressed after his bath, often in his siren suit; Churchill was well tailored but liked clothes that slipped on easily, the zippered one-piece siren suit at home, always zippered shoes. During the war he often lunched alone with Clemmie, again a hearty meal. After lunch he slept and bathed again, then settled to committee work. He had appointed himself minister of defence (there was no ministry) so that he might have direct power over the three independent service ministers. It was exercised through his remarkable principal staff officer, General Hastings Ismay, and serviced through his private office of five civilians, among whom John Colville was a key figure; so too was 'the Prof', Frederick Lindemann, an Oxford scientist, whose advice on technical matters he almost always took, not always advisedly. The principal means by which he directed the war was his 'box', a black dispatch case to which only he and his secretaries had keys. It contained the papers needed each day, arranged in strict sequence: 'Top of the Box' (vital matters), Foreign Office telegrams, service telegrams, parliamentary questions (Churchill regularly attended the Commons throughout the war), 'General Ismay' (chief-of-staff matters), and 'R Week-end', papers that required reflection. It was a strict rule that no instruction of Churchill's, based on reading in the box, had executive force unless written and signed. Urgent decisions, or requests for advice, bore a red printed label, ACTION THIS DAY.

The afternoon was devoted to meetings, usually with the five-man War Cabinet or the three chiefs of staff and Ismay. These might be prolonged beyond dinner, though the evening was usually devoted to more dictation. If Churchill was out of London, at Chequers, the Prime Minister's official country residence, or Ditchley Park, next to Blenheim, where he went to get away from the bombing, his small entourage would accompany him. Bombs, however, did not frighten Churchill. He went to Ditchley only if he wanted an undisturbed night. Often during the Blitz he slept in spartan conditions in a Downing Street basement, today a museum known as the Cabinet War Rooms.

An idiosyncratic routine and one that tried even those most devoted to him, it might well have irritated his fellow politicians. From the outset, however, Churchill's evident dedication to the single task of fighting the war, with the determination to win it, dissolved any opposition.

He found supporters whom Chamberlain had been lacking. The Labour Party, led by Attlee, which Chamberlain had declined to include in government, came across to him *en bloc*; so did the surviving Liberals. It was as a true national leader that Churchill assumed power. Attlee and Arthur Greenwood joined Lord Halifax and Chamberlain to form with Churchill the War Cabinet; a reconstituted over cabinet included Labour and Liberal as well as Conservative members. On May 13 Churchill warned them he had nothing to offer but 'blood, toil, tears and sweat'. He repeated those words to the Commons a few hours later. 'Nevertheless those words to the Commons a few hours 'Policy? I will he went on, rhetorically, 'You ask: What is our policy? I will say: It is to wage war by sea, land a

… You ask: What is our aim? I can answer in one word: Victory! Victory at all costs, victory in spite of all terror, victory however long and hard the road may be.' Though utterly heartfelt, his words partook of melodrama. Even as he spoke, the German panzer divisions were breaching the French eastern defences and beginning their breakneck drive that, in a delayed realization of the Schlieffen Plan of 1914, would achieve the encirclement of the French army – and the BEF – when their spearheads reached the Channel coast on May 21.

On May 17 Churchill flew to Paris in the hope of stiffening French resolve. He returned on May 22, to urge that counter-attacks be mounted against the neck of the German thrust. The French Fourth Armoured Division, commanded by the then unknown General Charles de Gaulle, had already bravely tried but failed; the British had tried again on May 21 and failed also. The Germans, with the then equally un-known General Erwin Rommel in the lead, were rampaging all over north-eastern France, spreading confusion wherever they struck. General Lord Gort, commanding the BEF, advised that it be withdrawn to Britain. On May 24 Churchill gave the necessary orders. An evacuation fleet was already being assembled. On May 27 it began to take the British troops off, from the harbour and beaches of Dunkirk.

In these desperate circumstances, with French units collapsing wholesale and the Belgian army capitulating altogether, Chamberlain and Halifax proposed to Churchill, within War Cabinet, that the British government consider seeking terms from Hitler. For a day or two even the lionhearted Churchill lent an ear to the suggestion. On the evening of however, when the navy had shown that

124

a complete evacuation might be successful, he rejected the thought. He told the War Cabinet that 'nations which went down fighting rose again, but those who surrendered tamely were finished.' A few minutes later he expressed the same sentiment to the full Cabinet: 'If this long island story of ours is to end at last, let it end only when each one of us lies choking in his own blood upon the ground.' In response to this Macbethian challenge, Cabinet ministers, Conservative, Liberal and Labour alike, jumped from their seats to shake his hand and pummel him on the back. 'Had I at this juncture faltered in leading the nation,' he later wrote, he had no doubt that 'I should have been hurled out of office.'

The Cabinet's sentiments were, it was soon made clear, those of the British people also. His instantly celebrated and perhaps greatest speech, to the Commons on June 4, in which he promised that the Germans would be fought 'on the beaches ... on the landing grounds ... in the fields and in the streets ... in the hills,' concluding, 'we shall never surrender,' evoked a surge of patriotic enthusiasm. The British remembered, and were reminded in every newspaper and broadcast, that they were an imperial and warrior nation, who had defeated every tyrant they had ever opposed and who were not now to submit to an Austrian house-painter (as Hitler was universally, if mistakenly, identified). The French might give in. The British would not. Churchill made a final flight to France on June 11, finding the French government in refuge south of the Loire, far from Paris. He tried to rally hopes of a counteroffensive from Brittany (from which he would shortly be forced to withdraw British troops in a 'second Dunkirk'), and of denying Hitler the fruits of his victory by waging 'guerrilla warfare on a gigantic scale'. Marshal Henri Pétain, the victor of Verdun in the First World War, who had been brought back into government, passionately objected that subversive resistance would entail 'the destruction of the country'. He was already advocating the making of an armistice with Germany.

An armistice followed on June 25, and Pétain would become head of a new polity, the État Français, successor to the Third Republic, with direct authority only over a 'Free Zone' in central and southern France, with its capital at Vichy, and the French colonial empire. Under Vichy, official France was to show no resistance to Germany whatsoever. Pétain refused to sail the French fleet into British ports as Churchill requested; as a consequence, in one of the most brutal acts of state policy of the war, Churchill ordered the Royal Navy to bombard it at its moorings. Fire was opened on July 3, at the French North African ports of Oran and Mers-el-Kébir, and twelve hundred French sailors were killed. Thereafter Vichy France treated Britain as an enemy. The proposal, raised on June 16 by René Pleven (to be a leader of postwar France), that the sovereignties of France and Britain should be merged so that the two countries could continue the fight as an entity, was forgotten altogether. The idea of French resistance was preserved only by General de Gaulle, who, recently appointed deputy minister of war, arrived in Britain on June 15. Three days later, in a broadcast scarcely heard in his homeland, he proclaimed the existence of a 'Free France' and urged those still at liberty in the French empire and elsewhere to 'rally' to him. Few did so. Though nearly two hundred thousand French soldiers had been evacuated from France to Britain in May and June, most returned to France. Ostensibly they went to continue resistance. Once back, however, they submitted to Vichy and to Pétain's rejection of any continuation of the fight by guerrilla means.

Churchill's belief that the defeated peoples of Europe could be brought to wear down Germany's control from within was to prove, almost everywhere, one of his most ill-judged ideas. On July 16, 1940, he instructed Hugh Dalton, head of the newly created Special Operations Executive (SOE), to 'set Europe ablaze'. The SOE was to lend support and supplies to the fighting groups that Churchill expected to appear spontaneously behind enemy lines, as they had among the Boers after their defeat in the field in 1900–1902. He had formed a warm admiration for Boer courage and intransigence (in fact, Churchill named the raiding forces he raised to carry war to enemy coasts 'Commandos', after the Boer military formations). However, his equation of the Boer War with the Second World War – and British imperialists with Nazi ideologues – was deeply mistaken. The idea of 'fair play' had prevailed in South Africa, particularly among the British conquerors. To the Nazis, legality and fair play were symptoms of democratic weakness that they gloried in affronting. Resistance was treated as illegal rebellion and put down by atrocity; resisters were sent to concentration camps, where most of them died sooner or later; those taken in arms were shot immediately.

'We have remained decent men,' Heinrich Himmler would assure his fellow mass murderers in his notorious speech at Posen (Poznan) in October 1943; 'decent men' were, to Churchill, either soldiers of the state or their principled guerrilla opponents. Rooted in public-school morality, he never anticipated the advantage that nihilistic amorality accorded his enemies – or that those who heeded his call to 'set Europe ablaze' would pay a terrible price for doing so. The severity of the Germans' repression aroused his most dramatic rhetorical strictures, but while the Nazis held the upper hand, his words counted for nothing against their acts.

The result was that in urbanized, law-abiding Western Europe most citizens were, understandably, too frightened to resist; they were discouraged from doing so, in any case, by the domestic bureaucracies that the Germans left in place. The brave minority who chose to sustain national honour by cooperating with the SOE did so chiefly by passing intelligence, printing illegal newspapers, succouring downed airmen, and committing sabotage. Where broken terrain, underdeveloped government, and a tradition of lawlessness toward foreign rule facilitated insurgency, as in formerly Turkish southern Europe, the Germans exacted a terrible revenge. Greece and Yugoslavia were ravaged by reprisals, and by the civil wars that resistance provoked. The suppression of resistance diverted little German military strength from the main war effort; of the sixty German divisions in France on D-Day, none was committed to internal security. The consequences of encouraging resistance in Yugoslavia and Greece were socially and politically disastrous; they persist to this day.

Churchill's belief in the power of resisters to weaken the Nazi grip on occupied Europe belonged with other flights of his strategic imagination. General Sir Alan Brooke, for most of the war his military chief of staff, observed that the prime minister had ten ideas every day, one good, nine bad, and that much of his own energy was consumed in discrediting the bad. They included a large number of schemes for diversionary offensives. Despite the spectre of Gallipoli, which had haunted his subsequent political career, Churchill was forever seeking to land troops on the flanks of the enemy. Norway was a favourite objective, though its geography would have doomed even a successful landing to frustration. Here Churchill's constant probing and feinting had at least the beneficial effect of feeding Hitler's own fantasy of a deadly Scandinavian danger, causing him to leave ten precious divisions idle in Norway throughout the war. In the Mediterranean, Churchill's passion for tangential operations had a largely pernicious outcome. Wrongly convinced that Turkey could be drawn into the war on the Allied side, in an abandonment of neutrality the hard-headed Ankara government expended acute diplomatic skill to avoid, he eventually insisted – against strong American advice – on invading the Dodecanese Islands, off Turkey's southern coast, in September 1943. The invasion was defeated by the Germans with humiliating ease. Defeat, or at a minimum costly stalemate, would probably have been the result of Churchill's later obsession with diverting troops from the Italian campaign to a landing in Croatia, aimed at Vienna, but fortunately it was firmly quashed by his American allies.

Yet Churchill's restless search for means to hit back at least had the effect of sustaining his own fierce resolve to achieve eventual victory, even at the lowest points of the war. In 1940 it yielded a priceless dividend, when he decided, though Britain lay under threat of imminent invasion, to reinforce its tiny army in the Middle East. In the aftermath of Dunkirk, the overriding priority was to defeat the German air offensive, in an epic fight later known as the Battle of Britain, success in which Hitler's generals and admirals insisted was the necessary preliminary to launching a Channel crossing. The Battle of Britain was hard fought to a narrow but decisive British victory. Even as it began, however, Churchill decided on August 11 to rob the garrison of the home islands of their last sizeable tank force and send it to Egypt, which Mussolini, who had brought Italy into the war on June 10, was threatening to invade. Egypt was the crucial link between Britain's European and Asian centres of power. Through it ran the Suez Canal, and at Alexandria was based Britain's Mediterranean Fleet, which Churchill had already decreed should not be withdrawn.

With the Mediterranean Fleet and the Army of the Nile (later the Eighth Army), Churchill controlled the means to take the offensive against Italy but also to disrupt Hitler's plans to extend his empire into southern Europe. He used both energetically. On November 11, 1940, British carrier-borne aircraft sank much of the Italian battle fleet at its moorings in Taranto (the attack inspired the Japanese descent on Pearl Harbor a year later). In December the Eighth Army fell on the Italians, drove them out of Egypt, and captured forty thousand prisoners, with much of Italian Libya. It was this defeat that prompted Hitler to send Rommel and the Afrika Corps to Libya to save Mussolini's face.

Hitler had already postponed indefinitely Operation Sea Lion, the invasion of Britain, and was preparing Operation Barbarossa, the invasion of Russia. Churchill's Mediterranean strategy, which extended to lending military aid to Greece, now prompted a further interruption. In April, Hitler launched offensives against both Yugoslavia, where an anti-Nazi junta had repudiated a pro-Nazi treaty, and Greece. Both countries were swiftly overrun, at great cost to the British force Churchill had sent to support the Greeks, but the outcome was to create a zone of insecurity on Germany's southern flank that would fester until the arrival of the Red Army in late 1944. Meanwhile, British troops, supported from Egypt, were dismantling the Italian empire in Ethiopia and Somalia.

Britain's small African victories did not weaken Hitler; indeed, Rommel was shortly to reverse the Eighth Army's successes in Libya. Nevertheless they sustained domestic morale and allowed Churchill to represent Britain to the United States as a nation still actively waging war. America's future strategic policy was now Churchill's chief preoccupation. On May 15, 1940, even before the Battle of France had gone irreversibly wrong, he had warned President Roosevelt that 'the voice and force of the United States may count for nothing if they are withheld too long.' Whatever Roosevelt's antipathy toward Nazi Germany, he was, however, the leader of a nation still strongly disinclined to intervene in a European war. The Americans, encouraged by the brilliant radio reporting from Blitzed London of such correspondents as Edward R. Murrow, came greatly to admire Britain's wartime spirit, but they were not yet ready to share its ordeal. Nor could Roosevelt easily move the American political class to help Britain with the war's costs. The supply of military equipment to Hitler's enemies was already beginning to liberate the American economy from the long depression; but the terms at the outset were to be 'cash and carry'. By December 1940 Britain had placed orders that exceeded its gold and dollar reserves, and future deliveries were guaranteed only against the liquidation of Britain's remaining assets in the United States.

In January 1941 Roosevelt sent to London a personal representative, Harry Hopkins, and through him a new basis of purchase was arranged: lend-lease, which allowed Britain to acquire equipment and supplies, particularly oil, against the promise of repayment after the war's conclusion. Lend-lease was, however, only a means of playing for time. Though it kept Britain in the war, it did not bring victory any nearer. Victory could be advanced only by some alteration of the terms on which the war was fought: American entry or the commission of some catastrophic mistake by the other side. Neither could be counted upon; the United States still lacked the motive of overriding national interest, while Germany and its allies and associates were playing a strong hand well. The future looked grim indeed.

What sustained Churchill, and the British people, during the second six months of 'standing alone', January–June 1941, now defies easy understanding. Bombing was killing thousands of civilians every month and burning out not only central London but also the centres of the provincial cities Bristol, Manchester, Liverpool, Birmingham, Glasgow, Cardiff, Belfast. U-boat warfare had reduced the individual's diet to one egg and a few ounces of meat each week. Clothing was wearing out and could not easily be replaced. Fuel for domestic heating was harshly rationed, like every other commodity. Luxuries had disappeared; alcohol was hard to come by; only tobacco, judged essential to morale, could readily be bought. The war was dragging out into an apparently interminable and cheerless future.

Churchill privately confessed to depression. The sinkings of British merchant shipping, half a million tons in March (out of a prewar fleet of twenty million tons) particularly lowered his optimism. 'How willingly would I have exchanged a full-scale invasion for this shapeless, measureless peril, expressed in charts, curves and statistics. This mortal danger to our life-line gnawed my bowels.' Robert Menzies, the Australian prime minister, recorded at this time that Churchill 'will steep himself (and you) in gloom', concluding, however, 'that there is no defeat in his heart.' He certainly communicated none to the outside world. Early 1941 was the era of some of his greatest speeches, made both to the Commons and to a wider audience, particularly and deliberately to America, via the BBC. Ed Murrow reflected that one of Churchill's greatest achievements as wartime Prime Minister was to have 'mobilized the English language and sent it into battle'. In 1940 he had swayed the outcome of the invasion summer with such oratory as 'Their Finest Hour'. In 1941 he worked indirectly on American emotions with his February 9 broadcast message to President Roosevelt about the 'mighty tide' of aid flowing across the Atlantic. The House of Representatives had the day before passed the Lend-Lease Bill. His speech concluded, in words to become almost as famous as those of his 'Never Surrender' address to the Commons of June 4, 1940: 'We shall not fail or falter; we shall not weaken or tire. Neither the sudden shock of battle, nor the long-drawn trials of vigilance and exertion will wear us down. Give us the tools and we will *finish* the job.'

That was grandiloquence. Britain, however well equipped

by the United States, had no hope of defeating Hitler single-handed. Realities were, however, of less importance during the 'standing alone' months than hopes and inspiration. The answer to the question of what sustained Churchill and the British in the darkest days is that it was his own words. From them the people took hope and Churchill drew inspiration. Bad at many things, Churchill had early made himself a master of language, and it was through that mastery that his career and self-esteem had been nurtured. By the practice of speaking and writing, particularly the writing of a heroicized history of his own nation, he had built up a great reserve of imagery upon which he now drew to forge what would indeed prove to be tools of battle.

Churchill's words did not only touch his people's hearts and move the emotions of their future American allies; they also set the moral climate of the war. Hitler, a mob orator, spoke little after 1939. When he did so, it was to utter threats and insults, glorifying aggression, deriding his enemies. Churchill, by contrast, avoided threats, condemned few (though Mussolini, for some reason, always provoked him to contempt). Instead he appealed to a commonality and nobility of sentiment that took liberty as its ideal and humanity as its spirit. He always spoke, moreover, as if the ideal of liberty, though particularly incarnate in wartime Britain, was shared by all who did not actively oppose it, in this way reaching out to embrace as allies, actual or potential, all those not on Hitler's side. Thus, in a broadcast on June 12, 1941, he sent out a

message ... to all the States or nations bound or free, to all the men in all the lands who care for freedom's cause, to our allies and well-wishers in Europe, to our American friends and helpers drawing ever closer in their might across the ocean: this is the message – Lift up your hearts. All will come right. Out of the depths of sorrow and sacrifice will be born again the glory of mankind.

Churchill's message triumphed. It was perhaps the greatest of all his achievements. In 1940 his words captured the hearts of his people. In 1941, and in the years that followed, his words drowned out the drumbeat of totalitarianism that had dominated the airwaves of the dictator years, revived belief in democracy among the downtrodden, inspired a new patriotism in the defeated, created a new confidence, and transmitted a promise of victory that was believed. Morally, Churchill set the agenda of the Second World War. Its realization determined, after 1945, the future of the world.

Churchill had to set a broad table. Bolshevism was to him anathema, and he feared and hated the Communist creed as fiercely as he did Hitler's. Nevertheless he recognized that, in a fight to the death, allies must be accepted wherever they appeared. When, on June 22, 1941, Hitler attacked the Soviet Union, Churchill was ready with the appropriate words: 'No one has been a more consistent opponent of Communism for the last twenty-five years,' he broadcast that night. 'I will unsay no word I have spoken about it. But all this fades away before the spectacle which is now unfolding. The past, with its crimes, its follies, its tragedies, flashes away … Any man or state who fights on against Nazidom will have our aid … It follows therefore that we shall give whatever help we can to Russia and the Russian people.'

There was little help to send at the outset and, as the

Wehrmacht cut deep corridors into western Russia, capturing soldiers of the Red Army by the hundred thousand, many of those close to Churchill doubted that Russia could be saved. He took a different view, offering odds of five hundred to one 'that the Russians are still fighting, and fighting victoriously, two years from now.' That was a euphoric view, in which he later faltered. It was nevertheless correct. In the summer and autumn of 1941, Hitler's soldiers overwhelmed White Russia, the Baltic states, and much of the Ukraine. As, however, the first snows of winter began to fall – 'there is a winter, you know, in Russia. For a good many months the temperature is apt to fall very low,' Churchill reflected in a broadcast the following spring – the Wehrmacht's advance slowed until, in early December, it halted just short of the objectives for the year: Leningrad and Moscow. The first Russian counteroffensive, which would bear out the substance of Churchill's bet, soon began.

Meanwhile Churchill was increasingly occupied with his own war. Its fortunes fluctuated. Pugnacity and readiness to help a friend in need were two of his salient characteristics. In April and May they led him into severe trouble in the eastern Mediterranean. His expedition to Greece, mounted with troops withdrawn from the Western Desert, resulted in a second Dunkirk. Regiments that had lost all their equipment in France a year earlier now lost it a second time. Units diverted to hold Crete in the aftermath were then overwhelmed by the German parachute assault of May 20, while the navy's effort to cover the evacuation of the survivors cost it heavy ship losses. In the absence of the British troops sent to Greece, Rommel mounted a desert offensive that reversed the results of their victory over the Italians and left a large garrison besieged at Tobruk. In compensation, a German attempt to lend assistance to the pro-Nazi Rashid Ali in Iraq was frustrated, the Vichy French garrison of Syria and Lebanon was displaced, and the conquest of Italy's empire in the Horn of Africa was completed. The balance of advantage remained, nevertheless, very even. Not until November would a new offensive by the Eighth Army drive Rommel back and retake Tobruk. The desert war, important though it seemed to the British public, was, in any case, too peripheral and small-scale to influence the outcome of the titanic struggle between the Wehrmacht and the Red Army.

Churchill's strategic sense told him as much, and during the summer and autumn of 1941 he tried hard to fulfil the promise made in his broadcast of June 22 offering aid to Russia. Hundreds of tanks and aircraft and thousands of tons of war supplies were committed to the aid programme, regular convoys to carry the materiel were directed onto the Arctic route, and the bombing of German targets was intensified. Unfamiliar weapons proved of little use to the Russian soldier, however, while Bomber Command's offensive against Germany was as yet insufficiently effective to do the German economy much harm. Bomber Command aircrew casualties in 1941 exceeded German casualties suffered in bombing raids. Churchill could read the signs. 'Though we cannot now be defeated,' he told guests at Chequers on August 30 (by no means a certain prediction), 'the war might drag on for another four or five years and civilisation and culture wiped out.'

Everything depended on America's abandonment of neutrality, and of that there was as yet no sure sign. Lend-lease – to Russia as well as Britain – was flowing amply, and the US Navy was inching toward direct protection of the convoys that carried war supplies across the Atlantic. Roosevelt spoke warm words of encouragement, and his personal relationship with the Prime Minister was developing and deepening. Even at its most heartening, however, his policy toward Britain remained that of 'all aid short of war'.

In early August 1941 Churchill sailed on the new battleship *Prince of Wales* to meet the President at Placentia Bay in Newfoundland. It was to be their second encounter; the first, in England in 1918, had not been a success. The assistant secretary of the navy, as Roosevelt then was, had described the former First Lord of the Admiralty as a 'stinker' and 'lording it all over us'. The boot was now on the other foot, and Churchill exerted all his charm to make a good impression. For a joint Sunday service for the crews of HMS *Prince of Wales* and the USS *Augusta* he chose hymns he knew Roosevelt would like: 'O God, Our Help in Ages Past', 'Onward Christian Soldiers', and 'Eternal Father, Strong to Save'. That was percipient. Both men had a taste for robust poetry, later in their partnership chanting together the strident verses of John Greenleaf Whittier's *Barbara Frietchie* ('"Shoot, if you must, this old gray head / But spare your country's flag", she said'). Churchill and Roosevelt agreed that, in the event of America's entry into the war, Germany should be the main objective. Churchill's party soon detected, however, that Britons and Americans, whatever friendly words spoken, were not marching in step. 'Not a single American officer,' Colonel Ian Jacob, Churchill's military secretary, wrote, 'has shown the slightest keenness to be in the war on our side.' The material outcome of the Placentia Bay meeting was disappointing: the drafting of the

Atlantic Charter, affirming commitment to universal ideals of democracy, and an agreement to demand the withdrawal of Japanese troops from French Indo-China and to warn Japan against making any further advances into the South-West Pacific.

Neither appeared to further Churchill's increasingly urgent desire to draw America into the war. During the autumn, however, Japan's resentment of Western efforts to restrain its campaign of imperialism in China and South-East Asia grew. The military government in Tokyo was now being denied by Washington the freedom to purchase strategic materials, including oil. Its relations with the United States, China's traditional protector, were approaching a crisis. The peace party in Tokyo was losing influence; the army and navy argued for decisive action. Admiral Yamamoto Isoroku, Japan's foremost sailor, warned that a strike against American naval power in the Pacific, though perhaps successful at the outset, would result in the longer term in a crushing defeat. His words were set aside. By the first week of December, Tokyo was determined to fight unless the United States lifted its embargoes. Botched diplomacy delayed the ultimatum. On the morning of Sunday, December 7, 1941, Japan's main carrier force struck the US Navy's Pacific Fleet anchorage at Pearl Harbor in Hawaii without any delivered warning, sinking or disabling seven of its nine battleships. Next day both houses of Congress declared war with only one dissenting vote. Recalling in his history of the Second World War how he felt at that moment. Churchill recorded, 'So we had won after all!'

9   The Big Three, 1941–1945

VICTORY LAY FARTHER in the future than he could guess and not as surely within the Allies' grasp as he told himself it did. The enormous productive capacity of the United States, on which the lend-lease programme had scarcely begun to draw, would when fully mobilized outbuild the factories of its enemies and allies combined. Its reserves of manpower would suffice to create the strongest navy and air force in the world, and an army sufficient to fight decisive battles in both Europe and Asia. Industrial and military mobilization would, however, even at an American pace of urgency, take many months to alter the balance of power. In the mean time Japan was on the rampage and the two hundred divisions of the German army were regrouping for an all-out summer offensive directed toward Russia's oil fields.

During December, Japan shifted the focus of its attack in the Pacific from the American fleet to the territorial possessions of the European powers in South-East Asia. The Philippines, an American protectorate, were invaded. So was British Malaya. Off its coast on December 10 Japanese aircraft based in Indo-China sank the battle cruiser *Repulse* and the battleship *Prince of Wales*, in which Churchill had voyaged four months earlier to Placentia Bay. Churchill was deeply affected. 'Poor Tom Phillips,' he lamented; the admiral had gone down with his ship. Worse was to follow. British positions in Malaya were successively penetrated or outflanked. By early February 1942 the Japanese stood at the gates of Singapore, Malaya's great trading city. After perfunctory resistance, it was surrendered to the enemy, who were outnumbered by its defenders. The neighbouring Netherlands East Indies swiftly crumbled. So too did the British defences in Burma. Only in the Philippines was resistance prolonged, and there by May the American garrison had reached the end of its tether. As spring turned to summer in the Pacific, Japan was establishing a strategic perimeter that touched the borders of British India and the approaches to Australia and embraced most of the ocean's western islands. Only America's retention of Hawaii, just too far distant for Japan to risk attempting a second Pearl Harbor, and a few outposts such as Midway, offered any basing facilities for a counteroffensive.

In Russia the Wehrmacht struck deep into the southern steppes during the summer, with its objective the Caucasus and the rich oil fields around the Caspian Sea. The Red Army's resistance collapsed before the power of the offensive. Mountain troops hoisted the Nazi flag on the summit of Mount Elbruz, the highest peak in Europe; motorized vanguards reached out toward Baku, centre of the Soviet Union's oil-refining region; and the Sixth Army arrived at Stalingrad, the great industrial city on the Volga River. Hitler had reason to believe that the final defeat of the Red Army was imminent.

In Britain, Churchill's war was transforming itself from a campaign of bold words into a battle of brute facts. After 1941, though he spoke often, he made few memorable speeches. Instead he travelled. He was now only one war leader among three opposing Hitler, and the others, Roosevelt and Stalin, were supplanting him in importance. The necessity for him was to meet the others of the Big Three face-to-face, as often as possible, so that Britain's importance as a combatant, diminishing as it was, might be sustained by treaty or diplomacy. Altogether he met Roosevelt eleven times during the war, always – except at Casablanca, Cairo, Tehran, and Yalta – in North America. He met Stalin once, outside Roosevelt's company, at Moscow in October 1944. Stalin travelled only once outside Russia, to Tehran. It was Churchill who covered the miles.

It was a wearying task. He had never cared much about his personal well-being. His medical history had been one of wounds and accidents in youth. His intake of cigar smoke and whisky, though it sustained him, would already have damaged a weaker man. Their effects are exaggerated, however. His whisky-and-soda, as intimates testify, was more soda than whisky, and most of his ten daily cigars were chewed rather than smoked. Nevertheless, in his sixty-eighth year, his health was beginning to fail. During the first of his long Second World War journeys, to Washington, DC, in December 1941, he suffered a heart attack. His doctor, Lord Moran, confided to his diary that the correct treatment was six weeks in bed. He recognized that to give such professional advice was impossible. The news that the prime minister had become an invalid would have a 'disastrous' effect on the war effort, 'when America had just come into the war, and there is no one but Winston to take her by the hand.' To tell Churchill the same would be equally unjustifiable, because of 'the consequences on one of his imaginative temperament of the feeling that his heart was affected. His work would suffer.' Moran therefore decided to keep professional silence and hope for the best. His hope was justified. Though Churchill would suffer recurrences of ill health as the war progressed, he immediately made a recovery sufficiently good to allow his arranging with General George C. Marshall, Roosevelt's chief of staff, the setting up of a joint command in South-East Asia, to proceed to Ottawa to address the Canadian parliament and, on his return to Washington, to agree to the creation of a Combined Chiefs of Staff of American and British commanders, which would become the instrument through which the Western Allies' war-winning strategy would be conducted. He returned to England via Bermuda, on January 15, after an eighteen-hour flight, apparently quite unaffected by his illness.

Yet there was more to trouble his heart in early 1942. Quite apart from the disastrous news from the Far East, that from the Battle of the Atlantic was also deeply depressing. Presented with rich pickings by the failure of the US Navy to organize effective convoys, the U-boats rampaged along America's East Coast, sinking hundreds of merchant ships in what the submarine commanders gruesomely called the 'happy time'. In February Admiral Erich Raeder successfully transferred his heavy ships *Scharnhorst* and *Gneisenau* from the Bay of Biscay to the North Sea despite frenzied British efforts to sink them. In July a large convoy code-named PQ17, sailing for northern Russia, was caused to disperse by the threat of German surface fleet attack; many ships were lost, and the northern Russia run was temporarily interrupted, to Stalin's expressed contempt. Churchill would, in August, have to defend his decision to suspend the Arctic convoy sailings face-to-face with the Russian leader on a flying visit from the Middle East to Moscow. In the interim he had returned to Washington on his second wartime journey to the American capital, only to be confronted while there by a humiliation almost as severe as the loss of Singapore. Tobruk, the desert fortress, had fallen to a new Rommel offensive. 'What can we do to help?' Roosevelt inquired sympathetically. He diverted three hundred of the new Sherman tanks to the Eighth Army as a token of support. Churchill, however, could read the writing on the wall. 'Defeat is one thing,' he later wrote, 'disgrace is another.' While Britain continued to 'hold the ring', its military credibility was failing.

In July, back in London, he was obliged to dissuade the Americans from their belief that Europe could be invaded in 1942. Roosevelt had sent both Marshall and Admiral Ernest J. King, chief of naval operations, to argue the case. It was a bad one. Everything lacked: men, ships, aircraft. Only reluctantly were the Americans brought to accept the facts, to agree to postponing the crossing until 1943, and to use the American divisions preparing in the United States for the invasion to mount landings instead in North Africa in the coming winter. Churchill's sagacity only aggravated King's Anglophobia, formed when he had served in the US Navy squadron attached to the Grand Fleet in the First World War.

There were other troubles in July. In the Commons a vote

of censure was proposed; although easily defeated, it was an additional trial at a time of trouble. There was difficulty in the desert war. The loss of Tobruk had robbed Churchill of confidence in his commanders there, and in August he arrived in person, after another long and hazardous flight, to choose new generals. It pained him to dismiss General Sir Claude Auchinleck, the sort of soldier he admired: tall, handsome, a hero of the First World War. 'It was like shooting a noble stag,' he reflected; but Auchinleck was tired and associated with defeat. In his place he appointed the energetic, abrasive Bernard L. Montgomery, with Harold Alexander, a military aristocrat, as his supreme commander. Montgomery began at once to change the spirit of the Eighth Army, stamping on signs of defeatism, promising success. At the end of August he won a defensive battle against Rommel at Alam Halfa. It was the first in what was to be a succession of victories. Montgomery's appointment was Churchill's best of the war. Not loved by equals, superiors, or allies, and often a trouble to the Prime Minister himself, Monty shared Churchill's bellicosity and impatience for decision. He, like his patron, was a war-winner.

On October 23, at El Alamein, Montgomery launched the offensive that terminated for good Rommel's ability to take the battle to the enemy. The German-Italian Panzer Armee Afrika was driven from its positions and then, in a hard-fought retreat, out of Libya into Vichy Tunisia. On November 8, a large Anglo-American army landed in its rear in Algeria, swiftly overcame local Vichy resistance, and turned eastward to meet Montgomery's vanguards. The final defeat of Rommel was to be delayed until May 1943, but it was never in doubt. The success of these Operation Torch landings tempted

Roosevelt to make one of his few overseas journeys of the war. On January 14, 1943, he met Churchill at Casablanca, Morocco, where, for nine days, the two leaders conferred over strategy for the coming months. It was agreed that the cross-Channel invasion could not be risked that year, but it was firmly fixed for early 1944. Meanwhile the American and British troops in the Mediterranean were to undertake an invasion of Sicily as soon as plans could be completed. Churchill made his way home by a circuitous route, which included a visit to Turkey – which he still vainly hoped to draw into the war – to Cyprus, where he met officers of the 4th Hussars, his old regiment, and to Tripoli, Libya, where he reviewed a victory parade, which moved him to tears, as great moments so often did. Moreover, as Ian Jacob noted, it was a vindication. 'The bitter moment in the White House when Tobruk fell was swallowed up in the joy of the morning.'

The Casablanca visit brought other rewards. An apparent reconciliation had been arranged between General Henri Giraud, the Allied nominee to lead the Free French, and Charles de Gaulle, whose haughty indifference to his total dependence on Anglo-American support for once amused Churchill. 'He himself is a refugee and if we turn him down he's finished. Well, just look at him. He might be Stalin, with 200 divisions behind his words.' Roosevelt had not been amused. While he and the Prime Minister had greatly enjoyed themselves, downing highballs or champagne in each other's villas, Roosevelt had been irritated to distraction by de Gaulle's arrogance. The damage was never really to be repaired.

And there was other, belated damage. Once back in Washington, the Americans recognized that the British had exercised control. They had come accompanied by a headquarters ship, which kept them constantly in touch with London, whence data was signalled to back up all Churchill's arguments for the policies eventually adopted. In retrospect the Americans perceived that they had been talked into persisting in 1943 with the campaign in the Mediterranean, not a decisive theatre, when their interest, strongly supported by Stalin, lay in a direct assault on the northern French coast as soon as possible. Casablanca was to be the last Anglo-American occasion when Churchill's standing as the hero of 1940 allowed him to prevail. Thenceforward the policies of naked power would increasingly count, and Churchill, whose military resources were declining, would slip downward in importance among the Big Three.

Churchill himself was weakening as well. His family had feared that the journey to Casablanca might bring on another heart attack, and, though it did not, he developed pneumonia on his return to London in February. He made a seemingly complete recovery but then subjected himself to a renewed round of overseas missions that would have taxed a much younger man. In May he crossed the Atlantic in the liner *Queen Mary* (which was on a return trip from ferrying American troops to Britain for the buildup of cross-Channel invasion forces), and in Washington he was able to confirm the Casablanca decision that the victory in Tunisia would be followed by an invasion of Sicily and then Italy. He made his return by air to Algiers, to assure himself that General Eisenhower would abide by this sequence. In August, embarked again on the *Queen Mary*, he sailed for Quebec and, in meetings with Roosevelt and the American chiefs of staff, managed to persuade them that the British should be given a full part in the Pacific campaign, while conceding that an American should command the cross-Channel invasion, for which the target date was to be May 1944.

The issue of the invasion of Europe was now driving Churchill into a corner. By mid-summer 1943 the Red Army had passed to the ascendant on the Eastern Front. The Wehrmacht had lost its strategic reserve of tanks in its ill-conceived attack at Kursk and would henceforth fight on the defensive. Stalin was consequently emboldened to demand greater and more immediate efforts from his Anglo-American allies against Hitler's 'Fortress Europe'. The Americans – by now the dominant partner in the Mediterranean, where in July, Mussolini was overthrown as a prelude to Italy's changing sides in September – were in full stride in their reconquest of the Pacific islands. Britain, by contrast, had lost the ability to win victories unaided. A sortie into the Dodecanese Islands off the Turkish coast – against which the Americans strongly warned – ended in disaster. Bomber Command's night offensive against Germany, on which Churchill had counted so much, was beginning to be matched in intensity by an American daylight campaign; the RAF's 'Battle of Berlin' would end in stalemate, as destruction inflicted on the city was exceeded in value by aircraft losses.

Only in Italy were Britain's troops engaged in a large-scale ground offensive; their campaign in the Far East was making no progress against the Japanese defenders of Burma. Churchill's emotions were now deeply embroiled in the Mediterranean campaign, as they had been during the First World War. To Anthony Eden, his Foreign Secretary, then in Moscow, he wrote on October 26, 1943, that the battle in Italy must be 'nourished and fought until it is won,' and that

Stalin should be told that Operation Overlord, the code name for the invasion of France, might be 'modified by the exigencies of the battle in Italy.'

Although the War Cabinet and its advisers, particularly Alan Brooke, were behind him, Churchill should by then have recognized the folly of persisting in procrastination over Overlord. That merely enraged Stalin, to whom the Italian campaign brought no advantage, though he detected that Churchill saw in it a means of intervening later in the Balkans, where the Soviet Union had powerful, and contrary, ambitions. Arguing for delay had the still worse effect of infuriating the Americans, who had rightly concluded that the European war could be won only through Overlord, the preparations for which Italy was now beginning to drain. To defeat Hitler as quickly as possible was now the Americans' chief strategic priority. They had few thoughts beyond that aim, except going on to defeat Japan. Unlike Stalin and Churchill, they were uninterested in the nature of a postwar settlement, having no plans to remain in Europe after victory. They certainly did not foresee, as Churchill already did, that Stalin hoped to push the boundaries of Soviet power as far westward in Europe as he could. In consequence Churchill's efforts to peg out the frontiers of a future anti-Communist sphere of influence, embracing as much of the Mediterranean as possible, appeared to them merely a reflex of Britain's traditional imperialism, to which they were as much opposed in Europe as they were in Asia.

From the Quebec conference onward, therefore, Churchill was increasingly to find himself the odd man out among the Big Three. The change of status was demeaning, however successfully he disguised it in public and from himself. It was

Roosevelt who had proposed the creation of a personal relationship, as early as September 11, 1939, and their exchange of letters (two thousand, eventually) and telephone calls had sustained him throughout the hardest years. In March 1942, however, Roosevelt had intimated that he sought to make a friend of Stalin also – '[He] thinks he likes me better, and I hope he will continue to do so' – and by the end of 1943 that friendship of convenience predominated. Roosevelt began to try to arrange one-to-one, and secret, meetings with Stalin. At the Tehran Conference of November 1943 the two leaders did meet without Churchill and, though Churchill also met Stalin alone, it was chiefly to hear harsh words. Stalin demanded to know if Churchill really believed in Overlord. In the tripartite sessions Stalin got the commitment to a May invasion confirmed, and a guarantee from Roosevelt that the name of the commander would be decided 'in three or four days'. In return Stalin promised to launch an offensive of his own to coincide with Overlord, but his strategy required that in any case. As Churchill had volunteered a proposal to move Poland's frontiers to Russia's advantage, Stalin left Tehran a satisfied man.

Churchill left exhausted. Though on his homeward journey he was to continue his conversations with Roosevelt in Cairo, where he also saw the Turkish president, the outcome merely confirmed Britain's growing strategic weakness. Despite the American President's urgings, the British declined to attempt a landing against the Japanese in Burma, while the Turks again evaded Churchill's efforts to draw them into the war. Outwardly he kept up his exuberance. By the time he reached Tunisia in December, the setback to his health that his family had feared all year occurred. He developed first pneumonia, then fibrillation. From December 13 to 26 he was kept in bed at Carthage, while heart and lung specialists were brought from London. Not until December 27 was he able to rise, and then but to fly to Marrakech, to recuperate in the Moroccan sunshine. Only on January 12, 1944, was he judged well enough to go home. He had suffered one of the severest of the many medical crises of his life.

Yet, except at the worst, he had continued to run his war, seeing de Gaulle, Eisenhower, and his own commanders, principally to plan the landing at Anzio, designed to unlock the Italian stalemate. It did not. 'We hoped to land a wildcat,' was his later verdict. 'Instead we have stranded a vast whale with its tail flopping about in the water.' Failure at Anzio, and withdrawals of troops to join the invasion force gathering in Britain, were to allow the Germans to sustain a successful defence of the Italian peninsula south of Rome until June. Not until June 4 would Rome fall to the Allies. By then the troops in southern England were embarking for Overlord.

Planning and preparing for Overlord dominated the thoughts of all Allied commanders in Britain throughout the first five months of 1944, with the exception of Churchill. He found other things over which to fret: the postwar settlement of Poland's frontiers, over which he had bargained with Stalin at Tehran; the Italian campaign as always; and the subsidiary landing in the south of France, code-named Anvil, to be launched after Overlord with American and French troops taken from Italy; the still-faltering British campaign in Burma; the bombing offensive. In the dark days, when Bomber Command was the only instrument with which the besieged British could strike back at their tormentors,

Churchill had been fierce in urging the concentration of resources behind its campaign. Now that the tide had turned, and even though the Anglo-American strategic bombing offensive was reaching its height, he began to sicken of it. As early as June 1943, after watching film of its effects, he had burst out, 'Are we beasts? Are we taking this too far?' His revulsion deepened in the invasion year, even though he celebrated the achievements of Bomber Command in a speech to the Commons in April.

The one thing with which he scarcely concerned himself was D-Day, as the opening of Overlord would be known. One reason for that was that he had been effectively superseded; control of the invasion was now in the hands of Eisenhower, transferred from Italy to be Supreme Allied Commander, and Montgomery, whom, in a late flash of executive authority, Churchill had had appointed as ground commander of the landings. Another was his continuing debility. In March, Alan Brooke found him 'desperately tired. I am afraid that he is losing ground rapidly.' On May 7 Churchill confessed to him that 'he was no longer the man he had been ... he would be quite content to spend the whole day in bed.' His medical condition, as Martin Gilbert, his official biographer, suggests, was no longer as much physical as psychological, the effect of fears, over which he brooded, about the outcome of D-Day. John McCloy, the American assistant secretary of war, whom he was showing around the ruined Commons chamber in May, recorded that he suddenly burst out about 'the number of his early contemporaries who had been killed during what he called the hecatombs of the First World War. An entire generation of potential leaders had been cut off and Britain could not afford the loss of another generation.' His fears were to persist. On June 5, 1944, the eve of D-Day, Winston, after dining alone with Clementine, confided to her in his map room, 'Do you realise that by the time you wake up in the morning twenty thousand men may have been killed?'

In the event, D-Day succeeded triumphantly, at a fraction of the cost in human lives by which Churchill had been oppressed. By June 12 the five bridgeheads – two British, one Canadian, two American – had been connected and consolidated, the early German counterattacks had failed, and the Allies were preparing to push inland. On July 25, after the British had largely destroyed the German armoured divisions in a series of battles at the eastern end of the bridgehead, the Americans broke out of it on the western flank, dashed into Brittany, and soon afterward joined hands with the British and Canadians at Falaise, having achieved one of the great encirclements of military history. A Polish armoured division had played a crucial part; a Free French armoured division was shortly to do so. On August 24 it, with American support, entered Paris; General de Gaulle, whom Roosevelt and Churchill had reluctantly allowed to return to France, made a triumphal descent of the Champs-Élysées the following day. The Germans, meanwhile, were streaming eastward to their own frontiers, harried by Allied airpower and with the invasion armies in hot pursuit.

The success of Overlord wholly revived Churchill, psychologically and physically. He was to be ill again, with a recurrence of pneumonia at the end of August, but only briefly. The restoration of his physical strength was such that, though now in his seventieth year, he was able to resume his travels with increased tempo. The other two in the Big Three scarcely stirred abroad, Stalin because his fear of flying, akin to paranoia, kept him at home, Roosevelt because he had begun visibly to fail. Churchill, by contrast, seemed now hyperactive. He was possessed by an urge to view the actions of the victorious Western armies at first hand, visiting Normandy in July and Italy in August; in both theatres he got as close as possible to the scene of fighting, watching artillerymen bombard enemy targets and, offshore on August 15, the debarkation of the Franco-American invasion force on the Riviera coast. His other visits had a political rather than personal purpose. Churchill was increasingly burdened by the fact that the successes of the Red Army, which had destroyed a whole German army group in Stalin's promised offensive of June in White Russia, would result in the Soviet Union's postwar domination of Eastern Europe and the Balkans. He perhaps now accepted that Yugoslavia, where Tito's Communist partisans were in the ascendant, would pass into the Soviet sphere, but he was determined that Greece should not, and he hoped that he might still ensure a democratic future for the Poles, Britain's guarantee to whom in 1939 had been the occasion of its entering the war.

That meant dealing directly with Stalin. In September he made another transatlantic crossing to confer with Roosevelt, first in Quebec, then at the President's country house at Hyde Park, New York; the chief outcome of the meeting was to establish Churchill's opposition to US Secretary of the Treasury Henry Morgenthau's plan to dismember and ruralize Germany after victory. At the end of the month he was in Moscow. There he and Stalin battled for nearly three weeks over Eastern Europe. Churchill initiated the bargaining, proposing 'percentages of influence', 90 per cent for the

British in Greece, the same for the Soviet Union in Romania, more equal percentages in Bulgaria, Hungary, and Yugoslavia. There was an element of jocularity in the exchange. After the figures had been written down, Churchill suggested the paper be destroyed: 'No, you keep it,' Stalin rejoined.

Over Poland there was no joviality, however. Though it was Churchill who had, at Tehran, first proposed the postwar readjustment of Poland's frontiers, which would prove so much to Russia's advantage, he remained true to the view that Britain had gone to war to defend Poland from aggression, and he remained loyal to Poland's government-in-exile in London. Stalin was determined to supplant it with puppets of his own and could not be budged. He was eventually to get his way, which could not realistically be refused with the Red Army then deep inside Polish territory. Churchill battled on; but the intransigence of the London Poles, who enjoyed even less international support than de Gaulle had done at the nadir of his fortunes, tried even his patience.

In December, Churchill enjoyed the last success won in his incessant wartime travels. He decided to spend Christmas in Greece, where civil war had erupted between the Communist and monarchist guerrillas following the departure of the German occupiers. He arrived to gunfire in the streets, some of it directed at the British troops sent to restore order. Empowered by his agreement with Stalin, Churchill put the weight of his authority behind Archbishop Damaskinos, who was committed to restoring the monarchy. He left the archbishop in the ascendant in Athens and, on his return to London, persuaded the Greek king to accept him as regent. It was his final independent achievement in wartime foreign policy.

The European war was now entering its terminal phase. Hitler's air offensive against London with pilotless weapons had been brought almost to an end by the capture of their launch sites during the Anglo-American armies' advance into the Low Countries. His effort to delay their assault on Germany had been defeated by the failure of his Ardennes counteroffensive in December. Winter weather alone postponed the climactic Allied attack. As temperatures rose in both East and West, the Red Army began its drive from Poland to Berlin, the British and Americans to prepare their crossing of the Rhine. The time had come for a meeting of the Big Three to agree on the last details of a postwar settlement.

The place chosen was Yalta, in the Russian Crimea, the summer holiday resort of the tsars. Churchill arrived there on February 3, Roosevelt a few hours later. The Prime Minister was recovering from another bout of illness; Roosevelt was clearly at his last gasp. The agenda chiefly concerned Poland, though its future stood as a token for that of all the Central and Eastern European countries then actually under the control of the Red Army or soon to be so. Stalin refused to admit the London Poles to the interim administration but promised free elections to choose a postwar government. That was the best Churchill could extract. He suspected, correctly, that Stalin had no intention of keeping his word, any more than he had over a joint declaration of intent to allow free choice of government in all liberated countries, including specifically Yugoslavia, by then wholly under Communist partisan domination. Another concession made to Stalin was the agreement to repatriate to the Soviet Union all of its citizens found by the Western Allies in areas liberated by them. The fate of these 'victims of Yalta' would trouble the

Western conscience for years to come. Stalin, for his part, gave in return only consent to the creation of a French zone of occupation in defeated Germany, and assent to the establishment of a supranational association of combatant powers, to be realized as the United Nations.

Roosevelt returned home from Yalta a scarcely ambulant corpse. He died on April 14. Churchill, despite a sense of defeat at Stalin's hands, continued the recovery begun since D-Day. He had told Stalin that he would have to face a democratic election soon, as Britain had two parties. 'One party is better,' Stalin had replied. Churchill seems to have believed that the electorate could not reject the victor of the Second World War. In March he journeyed to the Rhine, which the Anglo-American armies had just crossed. As the month turned to April, he learned of the deaths of Mussolini and then of Hitler. On May 8 the news came of Germany's unconditional surrender. That afternoon he drove through exulting London crowds in an open car, then addressed them from a balcony in Whitehall. His speech concluded the theme of his first address to the House of Commons on becoming Prime Minister five years, less five days, earlier. Then he had promised that his aim was 'victory at all costs, victory in spite of all terror, victory however long and hard the road may be.' Now he was able to tell the people who had so faithfully accepted his leadership, 'This is *your* victory ... Everyone, man or woman, has done their best. Neither the long years nor the dangers, nor the fierce attacks of the enemy, have in any way weakened the independent resolve of the British nation. God bless you all!'

10   Apotheosis

THE CHEERS THAT greeted Churchill on VE-Day in Whitehall, and wherever else he went in Britain in the weeks that followed, were genuinely heartfelt. He was supremely popular. That was a tribute to the man himself. The British saw him as the leader who had won the war. To his cry of 'This is *your* victory,' many in the crowd had shouted back, 'No, it's *your* victory.' At the same time the British accepted his tribute to them as right and justified. They knew they had done a great thing. Whatever their occasional and individual fallings below the nation's traditions of greatness to which he had appealed, they felt that they had indeed done their best, that women and men alike had braved the fierce attacks of the enemy, and that together they had sustained as a people the nation's independent resolve, in the interest of the idea of liberty.

Yet, though they willingly gave him a generous share of the glory that belonged to their victory, they had already decided that the leadership he had given in wartime was not what they wanted in the approaching peace. For all his early commitment to social reform, and despite his wartime government's enactment of an enlightened policy for education, Churchill was seen by the man and woman in the street as a reactionary. His reputation was anti-worker and anti-welfare. Detailed examination of his political record would have shown otherwise, but elections are fought not on academic analysis but on gut feeling. In 1945 the British political parties, Conservative and Labour (the Liberals having declined into insignificance), faced the first general election since 1935. The mass of the electorate, which included several million servicemen voting overseas, had decided it wanted a government that was pro-worker and pro-welfare. In July, after a three-week delay for counting service votes, the Labour Party was returned to power by a landslide. Clementine attempted to console Winston with the thought that 'it may well be a blessing in disguise.' He replied, 'At the moment it seems quite effectively disguised.' The Conservative representation in the Commons had fallen from 585 to 213. Labour had a majority of 146 over all other parties. It was empowered to enact whatever measures it chose, and those were to include not only the creation of a free National Health Service (which it is now overlooked that Churchill proposed in the last days of the wartime coalition) but a sweeping program of nationalization of services and industry, eventually to include the Bank of England, the railways, the coal mines, iron and steel, oil, gas, and airways.

Churchill had not helped his party's case by alleging, even while the Labour leader, Clement Attlee, remained his deputy in the interim government, that Socialism, as he always called Labour policy, was 'inseparably interwoven with Totalitarianism and the abject worship of the State' and that Labour 'would have to fall back on some form of Gestapo' to achieve its aims. Not only were the allegations extraordinarily insensitive – since it was the Labour Party's detestation of Naziism that had largely helped to bring him to power in Parliament in 1940 – they were also unfair. Attlee's party had doctrinaire economic views, easily seen in retrospect to be quite inappropriate to the country's long-term material well-being; its leaders, Attlee foremost, were, however, sincere libertarians and proud British patriots. Attlee had commanded an infantry company in the Gallipoli campaign. The man he appointed Foreign Secretary, Ernest Bevin, was to prove one of the most defiant anti-Communists of the early Cold War.

The Gestapo speech was one of the worst-judged acts of Churchill's political career. He wisely did not resume that theme. In the aftermath of electoral defeat, he returned instead to the two activities with which he had occupied himself in his barren interwar years, authorship and magisterial foreign policy pronouncements. In the last days of his premiership he had represented Britain at the final Big Three conference of the war, held in July at Potsdam, outside Berlin. Both Roosevelt's successor as President, Harry S. Truman, and Stalin took it for granted that Churchill would return as the reelected prime minister when he left for Britain to conduct his campaign; Churchill did so as well. Rejected by the voters – but remaining leader of the Conservative Party – he displayed characteristic resilience in defeat. At the pit of Britain's military fortunes, he had told one of his private secretaries, John Colville, 'controversy could be left to History but he intended to be one of the historians.' He resumed the role of historian almost as soon as political power had been taken from him.

* * *

The first of the six volumes of *The Second World War* was begun in March 1946, the work progressing by the method Churchill had perfected while writing his biography of Marlborough in the 1930s. A team of research assistants assembled the documents. He composed the text largely by dictation, often from his bed. 'He concentrated ruthlessly,' recorded William Deakin, his chief assistant. Churchill saw the history as his monument. Boxes of papers followed him wherever he went. The second volume was under way by 1947. The third was completed in 1948, the fourth and fifth in 1949–50, the sixth and last the following year. It was an astonishing achievement for an author who on November 30, 1951, entered his seventy-eighth year. There were inducements. The sale of American rights brought in $1.4 million, a sum that, for the first time in his life, freed him of financial anxiety and even allowed him to set up a trust fund for his grandchildren. The history was emphatically, however, written not for money, but to ensure that his vision of the war would become the accepted version. He had done much to achieve that from the beginning of his struggle against Hitler, since his magnificent speeches of 1940–41 had succeeded in bringing the uncommitted to recognize the Nazis as villains and the British as heroes in a conflict between tyranny and liberty of universal significance. The universality of principle was perpetuated in the motto chosen to preface each volume: 'In war, resolution; in defeat, defiance; in victory, magnanimity; in peace, goodwill.' The text bore it out, to a degree remarkable in a work of such length. *The Second World War* is a great work of literature, combining narrative, historical imagination, and moral precept in a form that bears comparison with that of the original master chronicler, Thucydides. It was wholly appropriate that in 1953 Churchill was awarded the Nobel Prize for Literature.

While composing the history, Churchill had also used his time out of office to speak around the world on the issues now closest to his heart, as the victorious champion of freedom during a world struggle: the avoidance of future war and the guardianship of liberty. Churchill is often said to have been a man of contradictions, and he was certainly fascinated by war and frequently inflamed by its challenges and excitements. At the same time, or in the intervals between his excitements, war disgusted him. Though committed to the strategic bombing campaign, as Britain's only means of striking back against Germany during the years of siege, he had been horrified by its results. Though eager to bring the enemy to battle by land and sea, he had shrunk throughout the war from the cost of amphibious landings on well-defended coasts; as a strategist, he subscribed to the long-established British tradition of peripheral operations and the indirect approach. As a student of the future he had long nurtured a fear of superweapons, now made manifest in the atomic bomb.

In the afterglow of his triumph, Churchill could speak with conviction of the necessity never again to subject the world to the ordeal of total war; he could also demand the world's attention to his proposals for lessening war's likelihood. His best-remembered speeches on that theme were made in Continental Europe, at Zurich in September 1946 and at Strasbourg in 1949 and 1950. At Zurich he suggested the creation of a 'kind of United States of Europe' toward which the 'first step' would have to be 'the re-creation of the European family' based on a 'partnership' of 'a spiritually great France and a spiritually great Germany'. His speech supplied some of the impulse to the foundation of the Council of Europe, set up in 1949 at Strasbourg, where, three and four years after his Zurich speech, he called first for the admission of newly democratized Germany, then for its full inclusion in the new Europe's life.

By 1950 that meant German rearmament and German membership in the North Atlantic Treaty Organization (NATO), founded the previous year. Churchill's advocacy of what is now called 'the European idea', though today often invoked to justify 'ever closer union' of the Continent's sovereign states in a truly supranational federation, certainly fell short, however, of what modern 'Europeans' advocate. His vision of a future world was tripartite. It was to consist of the United States, his mother's homeland; a democratic Europe equipped with consultative and cooperative organizations; but also the British Empire and Commonwealth, Britain's leadership of which precluded its immersion in European institutions. Moreover, all three elements in his world vision were defined less by shared ideals than by calculated opposition to what threatened their common values: the menace of communism.

Churchill, even while extending the hand of friendship to Stalin at the end of the 'year alone', and later colluding with him in the settlement of the future of Eastern Europe, had never diluted the revulsion he felt for Bolshevism. It had deep roots, going back to the First World War and its aftermath, when he had overseen the British intervention in the Russian civil war. His anti-Communism was, however, not historical but ethical. While he may not have felt quite the same detestation for Marxism-Leninism that he did for Naziism – their moral equivalence, measured in terms of organized inhumanity, had not yet been revealed in the 1940s – he had an acute libertarian awareness of Communism's contempt for such ideas as the freedom of the individual, personal rights of property, the rule of law, and the sovereignty of small nations. Hitler, he knew, had been a monster. Stalin, he suspected, was a behemoth, intent on imposing a soulless form of Russian imperialism on any people lacking the means to resist the steamroller power of the Red Army.

He found the inspiration to set forth his fears of the Communist menace in what is today remembered as the greatest of his postwar speeches but was also the earliest, delivered at Fulton, Missouri, on March 5, 1946. He gave it at the invitation of Harry Truman, in the new President's home state. Ever since Roosevelt's death eleven months earlier, Churchill had courted Truman, with little result. He had failed to secure an invitation to meet him before Potsdam and had failed to bond with him at that encounter. At Fulton he succeeded in setting an agenda for relations between West and East that was to determine not only Truman's own foreign policy during the course of his presidency but also the nature of the Cold War. The Fulton speech was Churchill's ultimate bequest to what he had already succeeded in defining as the 'free world.'

Though widely denounced at the time, particularly in the United States, as an appeal to return to the East-West antipathies of the prewar world, it was nothing of the kind. It contained a warning and it demanded a course of action, both based on the depiction of the Soviet Union as a triumphalist and expansionist victor state. It was, however, certainly not anti-Russian or warmongering. Churchill's analysis was coolly realist, his purpose 'to place before you certain facts about the present situation in Europe.' The principal fact was that 'from Stettin in the Baltic to Trieste in the Adriatic, an iron curtain has descended across the Continent. Behind that line lie all the capitals of the ancient states of Central and Eastern Europe [which] all are subject … to a very high and … increasing measure of control from Moscow. As a result, the outcome of the war in which the United States and Britain had been allies 'was certainly not the Liberated Europe we fought to build up. Nor is it one which contains the essential elements of permanent peace.'

If war was to be avoided, Churchill urged, and he insisted that it was neither 'imminent nor inevitable', the English-speaking world must assume a posture of strength. Recalling his warnings about the growing menace of Nazi Germany during the 1930s, he argued that the horrors of the Second World War could have been avoided had the democracies then shown a bold face to aggression; he appealed that in changed circumstances, and despite their feelings of friend-ship for the Russian people, they should do so now. 'I am convinced that there is nothing [the Russians] admire so much as strength, and there is nothing for which they have less respect than weakness.'

The Iron Curtain speech, whatever hostility it aroused at the time, determined the international politics of the Western powers in the postwar world. It laid the ground for the Truman Doctrine, the policy that Russian intervention in Turkey or Greece would be opposed. It laid the basis for the creation in 1948 of the Western European Union, an outline of a military alliance against Soviet power. It provided the logic for the establishment in 1949 of NATO, the medium through which, by guaranteeing American nuclear support for a system of European collective security, the Iron Curtain was successfully to be made the line of forward defence for the Continent's democracies during the next forty years.

On November 30, 1950, Churchill celebrated his seventy-sixth birthday. He was now one of the oldest members of the House of Commons, which he had first entered fifty years earlier, and was the veteran of fifteen elections. He was also still leader of the Conservative Party, which in February 1950 had almost destroyed Labour's great majority of 1945. The government survived only with the support of the tiny Liberal representation. In October 1951 he led his party into his sixteenth election. It emerged triumphant with 321 seats against Labour's 295. On October 26 he became Prime Minister for the second time.

Though for him a vindication of his peremptory loss of office in 1945, his resumption of the premiership was not, any more than his retention of the party leadership, universally welcomed by Conservative Members of Parliament. Anthony Eden, his heir apparent, almost visibly chafed to succeed him. Others quite simply thought him too old, even too enfeebled, to govern the country. Privately he gave promises of early resignation; publicly he continued to behave as if the Labour years had been a regrettable intermission in the saga begun in May 1940. There were, he believed, two great tasks still remaining: to solidify Britain's so-called special relationship with the United States and to seek an understanding with the Soviet Union that would lift for good the threat of a future world war. He therefore continued to travel, to Washington in 1952 to encourage Truman in his prosecution of the war in Korea and in the American rearmament program; to Washington again in January 1953 to congratulate Eisenhower, his wartime confederate, on his election to the presidency and to propose that they should together seek a meeting with Stalin in Moscow. The special relationship benefited from Churchill's voyaging. The attempt to re-create the Big Three did not. Eisenhower was unwilling to visit Russia, and with the death of Stalin in March 1953 the basis for a renewal of the wartime relationship passed.

At home the succession to the throne of the young Queen Elizabeth II in February 1952 stirred Churchill's romantic historicism. He genuinely mourned the passing of the shy, dutiful George VI. In the enthronement of the girl queen, he glimpsed both a reenactment of the coronation of the young Victoria, who had reigned over Britain's greatest years, and a re-creation of the Elizabethan age, from which so many of the nation's most potent legends were drawn. Elizabeth II's youth and inexperience kindled protective and paternal emotions. It was by her wish that he became in 1953 a knight of the Garter, a great but yet lesser honour than he might have received at the moment of victory, when it was suggested that he should have been created a duke, as his great ancestor Marlborough had been at the end of the War of the Spanish Succession.

His acceptance of the elevation and his persistence in the duties of high office concealed an inward decline. Old age was catching up with him. In February 1952 he had suffered a recurrence of the arterial spasms that had first afflicted him in 1943. In June 1953 he had a serious stroke, which left him paralysed on his left side. Lord Moran, his doctor, doubted if he would survive the weekend. He refused to give in to his symptoms, however, and, over the next four months, dragged himself back to health by sheer determination. 'This astonishing creature', Moran recorded, 'obeys no laws, recognises no rules.' By August he was again presiding at Cabinet meetings, and on November 3 he made a speech in the House described by the Conservative MP Henry 'Chips' Channon as 'brilliant, full of cunning and charm, of wit and thrusts ... it was an Olympian spectacle ... In eighteen years ... I have never seen anything like it.'

Churchill's successful return to centre stage had been assisted by the deliberate agreement of his colleagues and subordinates to conceal from the press and public the extent of his disablement. It was also aided by the incapacitation of Anthony Eden, who in April 1953 had been laid low by an illness that kept him off duty for several months; Churchill was actually substituting for Eden as Foreign Secretary when his stroke occurred. He was, moreover, to make a better recovery than his younger deputy. While Eden was undergoing repeated bouts of surgery, Churchill was continuing his composition of his *History of the English-Speaking Peoples* and undertaking new journeys to Washington and Berlin.

The shadows were, however, drawing in. During a speech to the House in April 1954, on his cherished theme of reconciliation with Russia, he was shouted down by the Labour opposition, while the Conservatives, apparently disconcerted by the undeniable evidence of his failing powers, did not rally to his support. His efforts to animate the Eisenhower administration met an equal lack of response. In November

1954 he was eighty. Gladstone had been reappointed prime minister at a greater age; Churchill now, however, appeared to realize that the time had come. In January 1955 he told his intimates that he intended to resign, and in April he did so. He had kept the Cabinet and Eden, his crown prince, guessing almost to the end. In the final hope of arranging peace talks with the Soviet leaders, Nicolai Bulganin and Nikita Khrushchev, he almost took back his pledge to go. On March 31, 1954, however, he informed the Queen that he would leave office in five days, and on April 5 he departed public life.

It was the end of one of the most extraordinary political but also personal lives of the modern age. His existence as a human being would continue. It was spent largely with his family but, outside that circle, often in the company of rich men who sought the honour of providing luxury for his leisure. He painted, yachted, enjoyed the climate of the South of France, where he had often been at his happiest. Ill health, nevertheless, dogged his last ten years. He had a second serious stroke in October 1956 and a third in November 1958. In June 1962 he broke a hip in a fall. He recovered well enough to make what would be his final visit to the House of Commons in July 1964, but it was in a wheelchair, and he was a sick and often confused old man. On January 10, 1965, a fourth stroke attacked him, and he died two weeks later, slipping peacefully away, surrounded by his family, Clemmie at his right hand. He was ninety years and forty-two days old.

The British people recognized in his death the passing not only of one of the greatest of their fellow countrymen who had ever lived but also of a supremely heroic moment in their own life as a nation. Whatever rancours he had aroused during his domestic political career were forgotten. It was resolved to bury him with all the splendour due to a warrior-chief. His coffin was taken to Westminster Hall, and three hundred thousand mourners filed past while it lay there in state. A state funeral was arranged in St Paul's Cathedral, the first to be given to a commoner since the death of the Duke of Wellington in 1852. Unprecedentedly, it was attended by the Queen; by tradition the monarch attends the funerals only of other members of the royal family.

Among the array of servicemen who paraded were soldiers of the Royal Scots Fusiliers, whose 6th Battalion he had commanded in the trenches. His coffin was borne by Grenadier Guardsmen, with whom he had served in France in 1915. Also in the funeral procession marched a party of cadets from Sandhurst, where he had begun his military career seventy years before. At the end of the St Paul's ceremony, concluded by the sounding of the Last Post and Reveille, traditional trumpet calls at a soldier's funeral, his coffin was placed on a barge and sailed up the Thames to Waterloo Station; the arms of the riverside cranes dipped in salute as the procession passed. From Waterloo the coffin was taken by train and road to the churchyard of the little Oxfordshire village of Bladon, near his birthplace at Blenheim Palace. There he was buried next to his parents. The grave was later marked by a simple headstone cut with his name.

It is today not much visited. Churchill's real burial place is in the hearts of human beings. Curiously, those who remember him most fervently seem more numerous in North America than in the United Kingdom. Winston Churchill societies flourish in Canada and the United States. At home his memory has been subsumed within something larger, the popular memory of the Second World War, which has been transformed into a national saga. 'This is *your* victory,' Churchill told the Whitehall crowds on May 8, 1945. With the passing of the years he has come to be believed even more. As the war generation ages, its survivors find themselves honoured and celebrated almost as Churchill himself was during the years of his leadership. Their obituaries fill long columns in the newspapers. The anniversaries of their victories fill the British calendar. Every year on Battle of Britain Day, September 15, ancient fighter aircraft, Spitfires and Hurricanes, fly past to thunderous cheers. On Remembrance Sunday in November the nation observes a two-minute silence; the Last Post and Reveille are sounded in Whitehall; and then the veterans defile in their thousands – sailors from the Arctic convoys, soldiers who fought at Alamein, the air crews of Bomber Command, parachutists in red berets, commandos in green, the firemen who fought the blazes of the Blitz, nurses, the blinded, amputees in wheelchairs, and the widows of men whose graves lie in Egypt, France, Germany, Italy, Burma, and the oceanic deep. As they march by, they cast wreaths at the foot of the Cenotaph, the national war memorial that stands under the balcony from which Churchill paid his victory tribute to the British people, until its base is hidden by a mountain of poppies and laurel.

The intensity of the British people's pride in what Churchill called their victory is the way in which they implicitly remember him. How *should* he be remembered? He was a strange man. Companionable, he had few friends.

Quick to display emotion, he evoked little personal affection outside his immediate family. And even there the record falters. A devoted husband and father, he was, by the account of his favourite and deeply loving daughter, Mary, in her 1979 biography of her mother, difficult at home and often impossible. Of his relationship with Clemmie, the most arresting memory Mary supplies is that she 'was absolutely unafraid of him.' That their private correspondence makes clear. Indeed, if anything, Winston was inclined to be in awe of her; certainly he was the first to make up a difference. But then Clemmie was a woman of great strength of character and unwavering moral sense. She consistently warned Winston against bad company – particularly the cronies she identified as false friends – and strove ceaselessly to keep his loose habits in check: his extravagance, his gambling. It is significant that she had few, if any, friends herself. Other women found her aloof, and her children, of whom she was passionately protective during their childhood, drifted away after marriage. Winston was Clemmie's only real interest, deep and lifelong. It was the nature of her interest in him that is so revealing, the key to much of his character.

She perceived at the outset his towering ambition, the ambition – as another of his biographers, Robert Rhodes James, himself a Conservative member of Parliament, has put it – to be 'in office and power'. Office seekers and the power hungry are, almost without exception, defective human beings and often dangerous to their fellows. Clemmie saw beyond the ambition to recognize the nobility of purpose that his ambition strove to fulfill. She saw that he sought to stand above the crowd not out of selfishness or vanity, but because he believed in the greatness of his country and the universal validity of the principles – above all that of individual freedom – that through the evolution of its long history it had come to represent.

The evolution of Churchill's own character bears out the trust she put in him. A rejected child, he found his first fulfilment in the excitement of soldiering. The bravery that he discovered he could display in close-quarters combat did much to restore the self-confidence damaged by his father's coldness and his schoolboy failure. His physical courage was remarkable and would help later to underpin the moral courage that was also a central trait of his character. Quite as remarkable was his early decision to transform, by self-education, his romantic vision of soldiering as a means of service to his country into a broader conception of public service, based on deep reading in history and political theory. Churchill never abandoned his love affair with war. At an early age, however, he came to see that there was an ethical dilemma in the military life, to be resolved only if it was dedicated to a higher good. The gratification of victory, which he enjoyed in India, the Sudan, and South Africa, he learned to see as a shallow sensation, unless victory was moral as well as material. In South Africa, in particular, he learned respect for the vanquished and concern for the welfare of the defeated.

His early political life was devoted to organizing a system of support for the weak who had been defeated by the harshness of industrial life. Churchill's reputation as a social reformer has now been so overlaid by that of war leader as to be forgotten. His commitment, however, was genuine and his achievements were considerable. Had peace persisted he might now be remembered, if only by political historians, as a pioneer of Britain's welfare state.

Peace did not persist, however. The onset of war in 1914, and the European catastrophe it left in its aftermath, determined that Churchill's life should take a new and decisive turn. In some sense the war years, and the interwar years that followed, mark a reversion in his life to an earlier emotional pattern: delight in conflict as a personal and national adventure, then solid plodding, particularly as Chancellor of the Exchequer, to repair the social damage war had done. The moral undercurrent remained, nevertheless, consistent. Bolshevism outraged Churchill's sense of political decency. Naziism, as soon as he perceived its import – and he did so earlier and more clearly than almost anyone else – aroused the same distaste. Churchill foresaw that Hitler threatened a new war and a total one; his experience of total war between 1914 and 1918 inflamed his anger against those in government who would not take the steps necessary to avert it.

When war came, Churchill at once realized, as even many of those he had made his political enemies during the appeasement years also did, that he was the only man in the country who could wage it with any hope of a successful outcome. After Hitler's titanic victories in May 1940, that outcome was doubtful in the extreme. Some of his own War Cabinet proposed seeking terms. As soon, however, as Churchill glimpsed the possibility of recovering Britain's army from France, he rejected the idea of a negotiated peace out of hand. From the 'miracle of deliverance' that was Dunkirk he resolved to create the basis not just for the maintenance of national independence but for eventual victory. It was a decision of extraordinary, almost irrational boldness. As a preliminary toward achieving it, he sent to the Middle East the best of what remained of Britain's disposable force at a moment when the home islands lay under threat of cross-Channel invasion. Once arrived, those forces were used in a series of long-range adventures – into Italian Libya, Ethiopia, and eventually Greece – designed chiefly to unbalance the smooth development of Hitler's grand strategy, not to protect any British vital interest. How Churchill escaped the probable consequences of his own recklessness remains a matter for wonder to this day; how he lived with the risks involved equally so.

By Churchill's own account, his personal coexistence with risk rested on his sublime belief in the prospect of eventual American entry. In retrospect that can be seen to have been much less likely than he told Parliament, the British people, and indeed himself. Neither in 1940 nor in 1941 was the United States in an interventionist mood; admiration for British pluck was one thing, joining the war on Britain's side quite another. Yet Churchill remained convinced that eventually he could, as he assured his son Randolph in May 1940, 'drag the United States in.' Why?

Oratory has strange powers. Churchill, not a natural speaker, had throughout decades of political life struggled to find the means to make his words effective in the ears of his fellow men. He eventually discovered the way to do so by writing his speeches in structured sentences and delivering them paragraph by paragraph. Their content was the product of his early years of reading in the English classics, by which he had not only taught himself the history of his own country but learned to relate it in the language of its greatest authors. When, after his youthful essays in journalism, he came to undertake the writing of history himself, he fell naturally into a recitative style, part literary, part rhetoric. As Robert Rhodes James perceptively put it, 'He wrote his speeches and spoke his books'; exactly so, for his books were taken down from dictation, which achieved the quality of magnificent oratory.

Powerful prose affects not only the reader or listener but the prose writer as well. The power of Churchill's prose reaches across the years, to touch me in a New York summer not long before his death, to move the grandchildren of those he sought to inspire in the invasion summer of 1940 six decades later, during the nation's mass and spontaneous celebrations of the victories of which he was prime mover. If we wish to know what inspired Churchill to become a great war leader, if we wish to know how he convinced himself that his mother's country could be made an ally, the answer is that he listened to himself. As he wrote his great war speeches in his first year as prime minister, he listened to the version of British history he had constructed in his head as a subaltern in his hot, dreamy Indian afternoons; he listened to his own apotheosis in biography of his ancestor, the first duke of Marlborough, victor over Britain's Continental enemies; he listened to his retelling of the story of the First World War as an epic of world crisis and eventual triumph; he listened to his recollections of his own youth and of the friends and acquaintances then retold in his lives of *Great Contemporaries* (1937); he listened to his own version of American history as an equal epic to Britain's in championship of liberty. Churchill spent much of his mature years remaking his life and experience in the form of epic. In 1940 events offered him the opportunity to make the present itself into an epic. He seized it with both hands and, through his extraordinary oratory, determined the victorious outcome of the greatest threat his country had ever faced and of the subsidiary and consequent threat to the idea of freedom – which was the inspiration of his being – in the Cold War that followed.

The essence of his magnificent life is captured in a speech he wrote to mark the unveiling of the memorial to the Royal Naval Division, of which he had been the founder, in 1925, long before the culmination of the horrors of the twentieth century that brought him to greatness:

> We are often tempted to ask ourselves what we gained by the enormous sacrifices made by those to whom this memorial is dedicated. But that was never the issue with those who marched away. No question of advantage presented itself to their minds. They only saw the light shining on the clear path to duty. They only saw their duty to resist oppression, to protect the weak, to vindicate the profound but unwritten Law of Nations. They never asked the question, 'What shall we gain?' They asked only the question, 'Where lies the right?' It was thus that they marched away for ever, and yet from their uncalculating exaltation and devotion, detached from all consideration of material gain, we may be sure that good will come to their countrymen and to this island they guarded in its reputation and safety, so faithfully and so well.

Occasionally and unintentionally men write their own epitaphs. Winston Churchill's tribute to the sailors-turned-soldiers of the RND may stand as his own memorial.

Sources

Beaverbrook, Lord. *Politicians and the War, 1914-16.* Vol. I. London: Thornton Butterworth, 1928.

—. *Politicians and the War, 1914-16.* Vol. II. London: Lane Publications, 1932.

—. *Men and Power, 1917-18.* London: Hutchinson, 1956.

Blake, R. *The Conservative Party from Peel to Churchill.* London: Eyre & Spottiswoode, 1970.

Bryant, A., ed. *The Turn of the Tide, 1939-43.* London: Collins, 1957.

—. *The Triumph of the West, 1943-46.* London: Collins, 1959.

Churchill, R. S. (Vols. 3–8 by M. Gilbert.) *Winston S. Churchill.* Vol. I: *Youth, 1874-1900.* London: Heinemann, 1966.

—. *Winston S. Churchill.* Vol. II: *Young Statesman, 1900-1914.* London: Heinemann, 1967.

—. *Winston S. Churchill.* Vol. III: *The Challenge of War, 1914-16.* London: Heinemann, 1971.

—. *Winston S. Churchill.* Vol. IV: *The Stricken World, 1917-22.* London: Heinemann, 1975.

—. *Winston S. Churchill.* Vol. V: *The Prophet of Truth, 1922-39.* London: Heinemann, 1976.

—. *Winston S. Churchill.* Vol. VI: *Their Finest Hour, 1939-41.*

London: Heinemann, 1983.

—. *Winston S. Churchill*. Vol. VII: *The Road to Victory, 1941-45*. London: Heinemann, 1986.

—. *Winston S. Churchill*. Vol. VIII. *Never Despair, 1945-65*. London: Heinemann, 1988.

Churchill, W. S. *The Malakand Field Force*. London: Longmans & Co., 1898.

—. *The River War*. London: Eyre & Spottiswoode, 1899.

—. *Lord Randolph Churchill*. 2 vols. London: Macmillan, 1906.

—. *The World Crisis*. 5 vols. London: Thornton Butterworth, 1923–31.

—. *My Early Life*. London: Thornton Butterworth, 1930.

—. *Thoughts and Adventures*. London: Thornton Butterworth, 1932.

—. *Marlborough*. 4 vols. London: G. Harrup, 1933–38.

—. *Great Contemporaries*. London: Thornton Butterworth, 1937.

—. *The Second World War*. Vol. I: *The Gathering Storm*. London: Cassell, 1948.

—. *The Second World War*. Vol. II: *Their Finest Hour*. London: Cassell, 1949.

—. *The Second World War*. Vol. III: *The Grand Alliance*. London: Cassell, 1950.

—. *The Second World War*. Vol. IV: *The Hinge of Fate*. London: Cassell, 1951.

—. *The Second World War*. Vol. V: *Closing the Ring*. London: Cassell, 1952.

—. *The Second World War*. Vol. VI: *Triumph and Tragedy*. London: Cassell, 1954.

Connell, J. *Auchinleck*. London: Cassell, 1959.

Feiling, K. *Neville Chamberlain*. London: Macmillan, 1946.

Guedalla, P. *Mr Churchill: A Portrait.* London: Hodder & Stoughton, 1941.

Jablonsky, D. *Churchill, the Great Game and Total War.* London and Savage, Md: F. Cass, 1991.

James, R. R. *Gallipoli.* London: B. T. Batsford, 1965.

—. *Churchill: A Study in Failure.* London: Weidenfeld & Nicolson, 1970.

Lamb, R. *Churchill as War Leader.* London: Bloomsbury, 1991.

Macleod, R., and D. Kelly, eds. *The Ironside Diaries, 1937-40.* London: Constable, 1962.

Manchester, W. *The Last Lion: Winston Spencer Churchill: Visions of Glory, 1874-1932.* London: Joseph, 1983.

—. *The Caged Lion: Winston Spencer Churchill, 1932-40.* London: Joseph, 1988.

Marder, A. J. *From Dreadnought to Scapa Flow.* Vol. I: *The Road to War, 1904-14.* London: Oxford University Press, 1961.

—. *From Dreadnought to Scapa Flow.* Vol. II: *The War Years to the Eve of Jutland, 1914-16.* London: Oxford University Press, 1965.

Moran, Lord. *Winston Churchill: The Struggle for Survival, 1940-65.* London: Constable, 1966.

Murray, W. *The Change in the European Balance of Power, 1938-39.* Princeton: Princeton University Press, 1984.

Prior, R. *Churchill's 'World Crisis' as History.* London: Croom Helm, 1983.

Skidelsky, R. *Oswald Mosley.* London: Macmillan, 1975.

Soames, M. *Clementine Churchill.* Harmondsworth: Penguin, 1979.

Spears, E. L. *Assignment to Catastrophe.* Vol. I: *July 1939–May 1940.* London: Heinemann, 1954.

—. *Assignment to Catastrophe.* Vol. II: *June 1940.* London: Heinemann, 1954.

Steiner, Z. A. *Britain and the Origins of the First World War.* London: Macmillan, 1977.

Taylor, A. J. P. *The Origins of the Second World War.* London: Hamish Hamilton, 1961.

—. *Beaverbrook.* London: Hamish Hamilton, 1972.

Wheeler-Bennett, J. W. *Munich: Prologue to Tragedy.* London: Macmillan, 1948.

Wilmot, C. *The Struggle for Europe.* London: Collins, 1952.

Woods, F. *A Bibliography of the Works of Sir Winston Churchill KG. OM. CH.* Foxbury Meadow, Godalming: St. Paul's Bibliographies, 1979.

Index

available from

THE ORION PUBLISHING GROUP

☐ **Andy Warhol** £6.99
WAYNE KOESTENBAUM
0 75381 381 5

☐ **Buddha** £6.99
KAREN ARMSTRONG
0 75381 340 8

☐ **Charles Dickens** £6.99
JANE SMILEY
0 75381 678 4

☐ **Churchill** £6.99
JOHN KEEGAN
1 84212 530 3

☐ **Crazy Horse** £6.99
LARRY MCMURTRY
0 75380 961 3

☐ **Dante** £7.99
R. W. B. LEWIS
0 75381 319 X

☐ **James Joyce** £6.99
EDNA O'BRIEN
0 75381 070 0

☐ **Jane Austen** £6.99
CAROL SHIELDS
0 75381 256 8

☐ **Joan of Arc** £6.99
MARY GORDON
0 75381 420 X

☐ **Leonardo da Vinci** £6.99
SHERWIN NULAND
0 75381 269 X

☐ **Mao** £6.99
JONATHAN SPENCE
0 75381 071 9

☐ **Marlon Brando** £7.99
PATRICIA BOSWORTH
0 75381 379 3

☐ **Mine Eyes Have
Seen the Glory:
the Life of Rosa Parks** £6.99
DOUGLAS BRINKLEY
0 75381 287 8

☐ **Mozart** £6.99
PETER GAY
0 75381 073 5

☐ **Napoleon** £6.99
PAUL JOHNSON
1 84212 650 4

☐ **Pope John XXIII** £7.99
THOMAS CAHILL
0 75381 703 9

☐ **Proust** £6.99
EDMUND WHITE
0 75380 918 4

☐ **Saint Augustine** £6.99
GARRY WILLS
0 75381 072 7

☐ **Virginia Woolf** £6.99
NIGEL NICOLSON
0 75381 147 2

All Orion/Phoenix titles are available at your local bookshop or from the following address:

Mail Order Department
Littlehampton Book Services
FREEPOST BR535
Worthing, West Sussex, BN13 3BR
telephone 01903 828503, *facsimile* 01903 828802
e-mail MailOrders@lbsltd.co.uk
(Please ensure that you include full postal address details)

Payment can be made either by credit/debit card (Visa, Mastercard, Access and Switch accepted) or by sending a £ Sterling cheque or postal order made payable to *Littlehampton Book Services*.
DO NOT SEND CASH OR CURRENCY.

Please add the following to cover postage and packing

UK and BFPO:
£1.50 for the first book, and 50p for each additional book to a maximum of £3.50

Overseas and Eire:
£2.50 for the first book plus £1.00 for the second book and 50p for each additional book ordered

---

BLOCK CAPITALS PLEASE

name of cardholder .... *delivery address*
.... *(if different from cardholder)*
address of cardholder ....
....
....
....
postcode .... *postcode* ....

☐ I enclose my remittance for £...............................

☐ please debit my Mastercard/Visa/Access/Switch (delete as appropriate)

card number ⬜⬜⬜⬜⬜⬜⬜⬜⬜⬜⬜⬜⬜⬜⬜⬜⬜⬜

expiry date ⬜⬜⬜⬜   Switch issue no. ⬜⬜

signature ....

prices and availability are subject to change without notice